o

Henri Maria Teresa

Raymond Reuter   Danielle Bossaert

Henri&Maria Teresa

Editeur	Luxnews s. à r. l.
Conception	Raymond Reuter
Photos	Albums privés de LL. AA. RR. le prince Henri et la princesse Maria Teresa,
	Bibliothèque nationale, Luxembourg; Tony Krier; Gérard Rancinan (p. 66);
	Tom Wagner (p.69, en bas au milieu); Arturo Mari, L'Osservatore Romano (p. 110 et 111)
Deutschsprachiger Originaltext	Danielle Bossaert
Légendes	Patrick Niclot
English translation	Raymond Kerr
Coordination technique	Théo Wanderscheidt
Layout	Dan Majerus
Lithographies	Reprolux, Luxembourg
Reliure	Ateliers d'Arts Graphiques, Howald
Impression	Imprimerie Saint-Paul s.a., Luxembourg

Imprimé au Grand-Duché de Luxembourg, 1997

ISBN 2-9599932-0-9

Les souverains de la maison de Nassau-Weilburg au Grand-Duché

Die Landesfürsten aus dem Haus Nassau-Weilburg im Großherzogtum

The rulers from the House of Nassau-Weilburg in the Grand Duchy of Luxembourg

epuis l'avènement de la dynastie des Nassau-Weilburg au Luxembourg, qui remonte à 1890, plus d'un siècle s'est écoulé et cinq grands-ducs et grandes-duchesses différents se sont succédé à la tête du pays. Entre-temps, la mentalité, la politique et l'industrie luxembourgeoises ont profondément changé. Le caractère de la dynastie grand-ducale s'est également modifié en parallèle avec cette évolution. ◆ À l'encontre des courants politiques qui ont notamment traversé les grands Etats limitrophes, l'institution monarchique luxembourgeoise ne s'est nullement affaiblie. Au contraire, elle est parvenue à s'enraciner de plus en plus profondément dans la société locale. Au même titre que l'histoire commune, le trilinguisme et la prospérité économique, la maison grand-ducale, devenue entre-temps luxembourgeoise, s'est affirmée comme un important élé-

eit dem Beginn der Dynastie Nassau-Weilburg in Luxemburg im Jahre 1890 sind inzwischen über 100 Jahre vergangen, in denen fünf verschiedene Großherzöge und Großherzoginnen dieses hohe Amt ausübten. In dieser Zeit haben sich die luxemburgische Mentalität, die Politik und die Wirtschaft grundlegend verändert. Parallel zu dieser Entwicklung wandelte sich auch der Charakter der Dynastie im Großherzogtum. ◆ Entgegen den politischen Strömungen vor allem in den großen Nachbarstaaten hat die monarchische Institution in Luxemburg jedoch nicht an Bedeutung verloren; im Gegenteil, sie konnte sich immer fester in die hiesige Gesellschaft verankern. Neben der gemeinsamen Geschichte, der Dreisprachigkeit und dem wirtschaftlichen Wohlstand hat sich das inzwischen luxemburgische Haus zu einem wichtigen Bestandteil unserer Stabilität

ore than a hundred years have passed since the start of the Nassau-Weilburg dynasty in Luxembourg in 1890, during which time five different Grand Dukes and Grand Duchesses have reigned. In the years of their rule the Luxembourg mentality, Luxembourg politics and the Luxembourg economy have undergone fundamental change. The same period has also seen a change in the nature of the grand ducal dynasty. ◆ Defying the political trend that has been especially prevalent in the large neighbouring States, the institution of the monarchy in Luxembourg has not lost any of its importance; on the contrary, it has become ever more firmly rooted in society here. Along with a common history, trilingualism and economic prosperity, the dynasty that has now become the House of Luxembourg is one of the main factors of our stability, an essential means of underli-

ment de la stabilité dont le «petit» Luxembourg, entouré de puissants voisins, a absolument besoin pour asseoir sa propre identité nationale. ◆ Le profond attachement des Luxembourgeois envers leur dynastie s'est surtout nourri des événements qui se sont produits pendant et après la guerre. Depuis le règne du grand-duc Adolphe, les facteurs suivants ont contribué de manière déterminante à cette évolution: identification croissante des monarques aux intérêts du pays et donc respect et défense active de ceux-ci, rôle exemplaire de la dynastie durant la Deuxième Guerre mondiale, adaptation harmonieuse de la monarchie aux exigences de l'organisation politique de la démocratie et de l'état-providence modernes, et discrétion des souverains. Rétrospectivement, il apparaît que les trois premiers chefs d'État – Adolphe, Guillaume IV et Marie-Adélaïde – ont construit les fondations sur lesquelles leurs successeurs ont réussi à bâtir des liens de plus en plus étroits avec leurs sujets[1].

entwickelt, der für das kleine Luxemburg mit seinen großen Nachbarn wesentlich ist für die Hervorhebung seiner eigenen nationalen Identität. ⬧ Die tiefe Verbundenheit der Luxemburger mit ihrer Dynastie konnte vor allem durch die Kriegs- und Nachkriegsereignisse gestärkt werden; seit der Herrschaft von Großherzog Adolf haben folgende Faktoren entscheidend zu dieser Entwicklung beigetragen: Die zunehmende Identifikation der Landesfürsten mit den Interessen des Landes sowie deren aktive Wahrnehmung und Verteidigung; die herausragende Rolle der Dynastie im Zweiten Weltkrieg; ihre harmonische Anpassung an die Erfordernisse der modernen politischen und wohlfahrtsstaatlich organisierten Demokratie und ihre Diskretion. Aus dem heutigen Blickwinkel wird erkennbar, daß die drei ersten Staatsoberhäupter Adolf, Wilhelm IV. und Marie-Adelheid den Grundstein legten, auf dem die folgenden Monarchen die seitdem sehr eng gewordene Beziehung zu den Luxemburgern aufbauen konnten.[1]

ning the national identity of little Luxembourg in relation to its larger neighbours. ◆ The Luxembourgers' profound sense of solidarity with their dynasty was particularly strengthened by the events of wartime and the postwar years. Since the reign of Grand Duke Adolf the following factors have played a vital part in this development: the increasing identification of the ruler with the interests of the country and with their active promotion and defence, the prominent role played by the dynasty during the Second World War, their harmonious adjustment to the needs of modern political democracy and the welfare state and their discretion. With the benefit of hindsight it is plain to see that the first three Heads of State, Adolf, William IV and Marie-Adélaïde laid the foundations on which their successors have been able to develop a very close link with the people of Luxembourg[1].

1 Christian Calmes, Le premier centenaire de la Maison de Luxembourg, Luxemburger Wort du 8 décembre 1990, supplément spécial, p. 1.

1 Christian Calmes, Le premier centenaire de la Maison de Luxembourg, Luxemburger Wort vom 8. Dezember 1990, Sonderbeilage, S.1.

1 Christian Calmes, Le premier centenaire de la Maison de Luxembourg, in the Luxemburger Wort of 8 December 1990, special supplement, p.1.

Le grand-duc Adolphe (1890-1905)

Lorsque Guillaume III, roi des Pays-Bas et grand-duc du Luxembourg, s'éteint en 1890 sans descendance mâle, la succession passe, conformément au pacte de famille nassovien[2], de la maison d'Orange-Nassau à celle de Nassau-Weilburg. Le duc Adolphe de Nassau-Weilburg (*1817 †1905), que Bismarck avait chassé du trône en 1866, devient grand-duc du Luxembourg. Né le 24 juillet 1817 au château de Biebrich am Rhein, Adolphe avait épousé en premières noces Élisabeth Michailovna, nièce des tsars Alexandre Ier et Nicolas Ier; après le décès de celle-ci, il se remarie avec Adélaïde-Marie, princesse d'Anhalt-Dessau, qui lui donnera cinq enfants. ◆ Adolphe régnera pendant quinze ans sur le Grand-Duché après avoir été grand-duc régent à deux reprises pendant la longue maladie de Guillaume III. Sa prestation de serment du 9 décembre 1890 marque la fin de l'union personnelle qui liait le royaume des Pays-Bas au Grand-Duché de Luxembourg et, avec le recul, le début du renforcement de la souveraineté de ce dernier. Son règne se caractérise par une grande adaptabilité aux institutions politiques et par le respect de

Großherzog Adolf (1890-1905)

Als Wilhelm III., König-Großherzog der Niederlande und Luxemburgs, im Jahre 1890 ohne männliche Nachkommen starb, ging die Erbfolge nach dem internen nassauischen Familienpakt[2] von dem Haus Oranien-Nassau auf das Haus Nassau-Weilburg über und der im Jahre 1866 durch Bismarck entthronte Herzog Adolf von Nassau-Weilburg (*1817 †1905) wurde Großherzog von Luxemburg. Der am 24. Juli 1817 auf Schloß Biebrich am Rhein geborene Adolph war in erster Ehe mit Elisabeth Michailovna, der Nichte der Zaren Alexander I. und Nikolaus I., verheiratet; nach deren Tod vermählte er sich mit Adelheid-Marie, Prinzessin von Anhalt-Dessau, mit der er fünf Kinder hatte. ◆ Adolf war 15 Jahre lang Großherzog von Luxemburg, nachdem er während der langen Krankheit von König-Großherzog Wilhelm III. bereits zweimal Herzog-Regent des Großherzogtums gewesen war. Die am 9. Dezember 1890 vollzogene Eidesleistung bedeutete das Ende der Personalunion zwischen dem Königreich der Niederlande und dem Großherzogtum Luxemburg und - aus heutiger Sicht - ebenfalls die Stärkung der Eigenstaatlichkeit.

Grand Duke Adolf (1890-1905)

When William III, King of the Netherlands and Grand Duke of Luxembourg, died in 1890 without male issue, the succession passed, under an internal agreement within the Nassau family[2], from the House of Orange-Nassau to the House of Nassau-Weilburg, and Duke Adolf of Nassau-Weilburg (b.1817, d.1905),

who had been dethroned by Bismarck in 1866, became Grand Duke of Luxembourg. Adolf, born in Biebrich Palace on the Rhine on 24 July 1817, was married to Elisabeth Mikhailovna, a niece of Tsars Alexander I and Nicholas I; after her death he married Adelheid-Marie, Princess of Anhalt-Dessau, who bore him five children. ◆ Adolf was Grand Duke of Luxembourg for 15 years; even before then, he had spent two periods as Regent of Luxembourg during the long illness of the King and Grand Duke William III. His inauguration on 9 December

■ Le grand-duc Adolphe

▨ Großherzog Adolf

■ Grand Duke Adolf

---

2   L'accession au trône d'une femme était exclue par principe.

2   Eine weibliche Erbfolge war in der Regel ausgeschlossen.

2   Female succession was essentially ruled out.

la neutralité du pays. Déjà âgé de 73 ans au moment de son avènement, le grand-duc abandonnera une grande partie de la gestion politique au ministre d'État de l'époque, Paul Eyschen (*1841 †1915), en qui il avait toute confiance. ◆ Avec l'accession au trône d'Adolphe, le pays devient aussi, pour la première fois depuis sa création lors du Congrès de Vienne de 1815, la résidence officielle du grand-duc et de sa famille. À compter de ce jour, les chefs d'État grand-ducaux n'allaient plus gouverner depuis la lointaine La Haye, mais au Luxembourg même. Cette proximité entre la famille grand-ducale et la population a favorisé l'intégration de la maison de Nassau-Weilburg dans la société luxembourgeoise, surtout à partir du règne de Marie-Adélaïde. ◆ C'est sous Adolphe, qui résida temporairement à Königstein et à Hohenburg, que le palais de la capitale, la résidence de Walferdange et le château de Colmar-Berg furent restaurés et adaptés aux besoins de la nouvelle dynastie.

Seine Herrschaft charakterisiert sich durch eine große Anpassungsfähigkeit an die politischen Institutionen des Landes und durch die Respektierung der Neutralität. Der bei seinem Amtsantritt bereits 73jährige Großherzog überließ einen großen Teil der Regierungsgeschäfte dem damaligen Staatsminister Paul Eyschen (*1841 †1915), der sein volles Vertrauen besaß. ◆ Mit der Thronbesteigung von Adolf wurde das Land erstmals seit seiner Schaffung auf dem Wiener Kongreß im Jahre 1815 zur offiziellen Residenz des Großherzogs und seiner Familie. Seitdem übten die luxemburgischen Staatsoberhäupter ihr Amt nicht mehr im fernen Den Haag aus, sondern in Luxemburg. Diese Nähe der großherzoglichen Familie zu der Bevölkerung hat besonders seit Marie-Adelheid die Integration des Hauses Nassau-Weilburg in die luxemburgische Gemeinschaft erleichtert. ◆ Unter Großherzog Adolf, der zeitweise in Königstein und Hohenburg residierte, wurden das hauptstädtische Palais, die Residenz in Walferdingen und das Schloß von Colmar-Berg restauriert und den Bedürfnissen der neuen Dynastie angepaßt.

1890 marked the end of the personal union between the Kingdom of the Netherlands and the Grand Duchy of Luxembourg and also – as we can see today – strengthened its autonomy. What characterized Adolf's rule was his great ability to adapt to the political institutions of the country and to preserve neutrality. The Grand Duke, who was already 73 years old when he took office, delegated much of the business of government to his Minister of State, Paul Eyschen (b.1841, d.1915), whom he trusted implicitly. ◆ Adolf's accession to the throne meant that, for the first time since the creation of the country at the Congress of Vienna in 1815, a Grand Duke and his family had established their official residence in Luxembourg. From that time on the Luxembourg Heads of State no longer held court in far-off The Hague but in Luxembourg. This closeness of the grand-ducal family to the population has facilitated the integration of the House of Nassau-Weilburg into the Luxembourg community, especially since the time of Marie-Adélaïde. ◆ Under Adolf, who resided at various times in Königstein and Hohenburg, the palace in the capital, the residence in Walferdingen and the Château de Berg in Colmar were restored and adapted to meet the needs of the new dynasty.

Le grand-duc
Guillaume IV
et la grande-
duchesse
Marie-Anne

Großherzog
Wilhelm IV. und
Großherzogin
Maria-Anna

Grand Duke
William IV and
Grand Duchess
Maria-Anna

■ Le grand-duc Guillaume IV (1905-1912)

Guillaume IV (*1852 †1912) succède sur le trône à son père Adolphe
en 1905. Son court règne, qui
s'étend sur une période de sept ans,
est assombri d'emblée par la maladie du souverain. En 1893, il épouse
l'infante du Portugal, la princesse
catholique Marie-Anne de Bra-
gance, qui lui donne six filles.
Guillaume n'ayant pas de descend-
ant mâle, la maison régnante pro-

■ Großherzog Wilhelm IV. (1905-1912)

Wilhelm IV. (*1852 †1912) folgte
seinem Vater Adolf im Jahre 1905
auf den Thron. Seine kurze Herrschaft, die sich über sieben Jahre
erstreckte, wurde von Anfang an von
seiner Krankheit überschattet. Im
Jahre 1893 heiratete er die Infantin
von Portugal, die katholische Prinzessin Maria-Anna von Braganza,
die ihm sechs Töchter schenkte.
Weil Wilhelm keine männlichen

■ Grand Duke William IV (1905-1912)

William IV (b.1852, d.1912) succeeded his father Adolf on the
throne in 1905. His short reign, las-
ting only seven years, was dogged by
ill-health from the outset. In 1893
he married the Portuguese Infanta,
the Catholic princess Maria-Anna
de Bragança, who bore him six
daughters. Since William had no
male heirs, the Protestant House of
Nassau-Weilburg became a Catholic

testante de Nassau-Weilburg se transforme en dynastie catholique[3] et sa fille aînée, Marie-Adélaïde, deviendra la première grande-duchesse élevée dans la foi catholique. Dès avril 1908, l'épouse de Guillaume devient d'abord gouverneur puis, en octobre de la même année, régente du Grand-Duché. ◆ Comme son père, Guillaume évita de se mêler des affaires politiques du gouvernement. Il perpétuait ainsi une tradition qui ne s'est jamais interrompue jusqu'ici, si ce n'est brièvement sous le règne de Marie-Adélaïde. ◆ Du point de vue de l'intégration graduelle de la maison de Nassau-Weilburg à la société luxembourgeoise, le fait marquant du règne de Guillaume IV est l'établissement définitif de la famille grand-ducale au Luxembourg. Les filles du grand-duc, les futures grandes-duchesses Marie-Adélaïde et Charlotte, deviendront ainsi les premières souveraines luxembourgeoises à être nées et à avoir grandi dans le pays depuis le Moyen-Âge.

Nachfolger hatte, wurde aus dem protestantischen Fürstenhaus Nassau-Weilburg eine katholische Dynastie[3], und Marie-Adelheid, seine älteste Tochter, wird die erste im katholischen Glauben erzogene Großherzogin sein. Bereits im April 1908 wurde die Gemahlin von Wilhelm zuerst seine Statthalterin und im November desselben Jahres Regentin des Großherzogs. Wie sein Vater mischte sich auch Wilhelm nicht in die politischen Geschäfte der Regierung ein. Damit setzte er eine Tradition fort, die bis heute lediglich für kurze Zeit von der Großherzogin Marie-Adelheid unterbrochen wurde. Mit Blick auf die allmähliche Verankerung des Hauses Nassau-Weilburg in die luxemburgische Gesellschaft ist von Bedeutung, daß die großherzogliche Familie unter der Herrschaft von Wilhelm IV. endgültig in Luxemburg seßhaft wurde. Seine Töchter, die zukünftigen Großherzoginnen Marie-Adelheid und Charlotte, werden somit die ersten Staatsoberhäupter seit dem Mittelalter sein, die im Lande geboren und aufgewachsen sind.

dynasty[3], and Marie-Adélaïde, his eldest daughter, was to be the first Grand Duchess reared in the Catholic faith. ◆ By April 1908 Maria-Anna had become Governess of the Grand Duchy, and in November of the same year she was appointed Regent. Like his father, William refrained from interfering in the political business of the Government, thereby continuing a tradition that has lasted until the present day with only a brief interruption in the reign of Grand Duchess Marie-Adélaïde. ◆ In the context of the gradual embedding of the House of Nassau-Weilburg into Luxembourg society, it is significant that the grand-ducal family finally became permanently resident in Luxembourg during the reign of William IV. Two of his daughters, the future Grand Duchesses Marie-Adélaïde and Charlotte, were thus to become the first sovereigns since the Middle Ages to be born and brought up in Luxembourg.

---

3 Comme tous les ducs de Nassau, Guillaume IV était protestant. Lors de son mariage avec la princesse catholique, il avait été convenu que toutes les filles du couple seraient élevées dans la religion de leur mère alors que les fils seraient éduqués dans la foi de leur père.

3 Wilhelm IV. war wie alle Herzöge von Nassau protestantisch. Bei seiner Heirat mit der katholischen Prinzessin war vereinbart worden, daß alle Töchter nach der Religion der Mutter erzogen werden sollten, während die Söhne den Glauben des Vaters annehmen sollten.

3 William IV, like all the Dukes of Nassau, was a Protestant. When he married the Catholic princess an agreement was concluded that all daughters would be brought up in the religion of their mother, while all sons would be brought up in their father's faith.

La grande-duchesse Marie-Adélaïde (1912-1919)

Un peu avant sa mort en 1912, le grand-duc Guillaume IV avait fait voter par la Chambre des députés un nouveau statut de famille aux termes duquel les femmes pouvaient également prétendre à la succession. Cette disposition allait permettre à l'aînée de ses six filles, Marie-Adélaïde, de lui succéder sur le trône sous la régence de sa mère, la grande-duchesse Marie-Anne, dans un premier temps. ◆ Le règne de Marie-Adélaïde (*1894 †1924), âgée de 18 ans à peine lors de son accession au trône, prend place dans une période difficile et conflictuelle de l'histoire luxembourgeoise. Il fut marqué par les luttes entre catholiques et libéraux pour la conquête du pouvoir, par les événements de la Première Guerre mondiale et par les visées annexionnistes françaises et surtout belges. La monarchie elle-même sera confrontée à sa crise de légitimité la plus grave, dont elle sortira pourtant renforcée à la suite du référendum du 28 septembre 1919. Quelque 80% des Luxembourgeois s'y prononcèrent pour le maintien de la dynastie sous la conduite de la grande-duchesse Charlotte et, du même coup, pour la subsistance d'un état Luxembourgeois indépendant. À

Großherzogin Marie-Adelheid (1912-1919)

Großherzog Wilhelm IV. hatte noch rechtzeitig vor seinem Tod im Jahre 1912 ein neues Familienstatut in der Abgeordnetenkammer einbringen lassen, nach dem auch weibliche Familienmitglieder die Thronfolge antreten können. Durch diese Regelung konnte die älteste seiner sechs Töchter, Marie-Adelheid, - zuerst unter der Regentschaft ihrer Mutter, der Großherzogin Maria-Anna - dem Vater auf den Thron folgen. Die Herrschaft der bei ihrem Amtsantritt erst 18 Jahre alten Marie-Adelheid (*1894 †1924) fiel in eine schwierige, konfliktgeladene Periode der luxemburgischen Geschichte. Sie wurde von den innenpolitischen Machtkämpfen zwischen den Katholiken und den Liberalen, den Ereignissen des Ersten Weltkrieges und den Bedrängnissen des französischen und insbesondere belgischen Annexionismus geprägt. Die Dynastie selbst stand vor ihrer schwierigsten Bewährungsprobe, aus der sie jedoch nach dem Referendum vom 28. September 1919 gestärkt hervorging. In dieser Volksbefragung hatten sich rund 80% der Luxemburger für die Beibehaltung der Dynastie unter der Großherzogin Charlotte und somit für die Aufrechterhaltung eines unabhängigen

Grand Duchess Marie-Adélaïde (1912-1919)

Shortly before his death in 1912, Grand Duke William IV had made arrangements for a new Bill of Succession to be introduced in the Chamber of Deputies, whereby female family members could also accede to the throne. This new system enabled the eldest of his six daughters, Marie-Adélaïde – initially under the regency of her mother, Grand Duchess Maria-Anna, to succeed her father on the throne. ◆ The reign of Marie-Adélaïde (b.1894,

■ La grande-duchesse Marie-Adélaïde

Großherzogin Marie-Adelheid

■ Grand Duchess Marie-Adélaïde

partir de ce moment, la maison régnante du Grand-Duché ne doit plus son existence à la volonté des grandes puissances; sa légitimité découle directement de la volonté du peuple. ◆ Le problème était que la grande-duchesse Marie-Adélaïde interprétait d'une manière excessivement large ses prérogatives constitutionnelles, comme la nomination des fonctionnaires et des bourgmestres ou la dissolution de la Chambre, sans pour autant outrepasser ses compétences légales. Après plusieurs décennies de discrétion politique du chef de l'État, l'intervention active de la grande-duchesse dans la culture politique luxembourgeoise était devenue proprement intolérable. Les successeurs de Marie-Adélaïde en reviendront ensuite à veiller scrupuleusement au maintien et au respect de l'impartialité de la fonction grand-

■ Les grandes-
duchesses
Marie-Adélaïde,
Marie-Anne
et Adélaïde-Marie

▨ Die Großherzoginnen
Marie-Adelheid,
Maria-Anna und
Adelheid-Marie

■ Grand Duchesses
Marie-Adélaïde,
Maria-Anna and
Adélaïde-Marie

■ Les princesses Marie-Adélaïde, Charlotte et Hilda
▨ Die Prinzessinnen Marie-Adelheid, Charlotte und Hilda
■ Princesses Marie-Adélaïde, Charlotte and Hilda

Staates Luxemburg entschieden. Seitdem muß das Luxemburger Fürstenhaus seine Existenz in Luxemburg nicht mehr auf den Willen der Großmächte stützen, sondern seine Legitimation geht unmittelbar aus dem Volkswillen hervor. ◆ Das Problem bestand darin, daß Großherzogin Marie-Adelheid die ihr zustehenden verfassungsmäßigen Vorrechte, wie die Ernennung von Beamten und Bürgermeistern und die Auflösung der Kammer, äußerst großzügig auslegte, ohne dabei jedoch ihre rechtlichen Kompetenzen zu übertreten. Nach einer jahrzehntelangen politischen Zurückhaltung des Staatsoberhauptes war diese aktive Präsenz der Großherzogin in der politischen Kultur Luxemburgs geradezu unannehmbar geworden. Ihre Nachfolger werden wieder strengstens darauf achten, die Überparteilichkeit des Amtes zu wahren

d.1924), who was only 18 years old on her accession, coincided with a difficult, strife-laden period of Luxembourg's history, marked by internal political power struggles between the Catholic and Liberal factions, the events of the First World War and by French and above all Belgian annexationism. The dynasty itself faced its most difficult test, from which it would emerge strengthened, however, after the referendum of 28 September 1919, in which about 80% of the citizens of Luxembourg voted to retain the dynasty under Grand Duchess Charlotte and hence to preserve the independence of Luxembourg. From then on, the ruling House of Luxembourg no longer depended for its existence on the goodwill of the great powers but drew its legitimacy directly from the will of the people. ◆ In the meantime, however, the problem was that Grand Duchess Marie-Adélaïde took a very broad view of her constitutional prerogatives, such as the appointment of senior civil servants and mayors and the dissolution of representative bodies, without actually overstepping her authority. After decades of political restraint on the part of the ruling House, this active involvement of the Grand Duchess in the political life of Luxembourg came to be regarded as nothing less than an intolerable intrusion. Her successors

ducale. Cette grande faculté d'adaptation à une société luxembourgeoise en voie de démocratisation progressive allait devenir, sous la grande-duchesse Charlotte et le grand-duc Jean, un des traits essentiels de la dynastie au pouvoir. ◆ La grande-duchesse Marie-Adélaïde abdiqua en 1919 dans un climat insurrectionnel. Son isolement politique intérieur et extérieur avait rendu sa position intenable, même si, constitutionnellement, la responsabilité politique incombait aux membres du gouvernement.

und zu respektieren. Diese hohe Anpassungsfähigkeit an eine sich allmählich demokratisierende luxemburgische Gesellschaft entwickelte sich unter Großherzogin Charlotte und Großherzog Jean zu einem herausragenden Merkmal der hiesigen Dynastie. In einem aufrührerischen Klima dankte Großherzogin Marie-Adelheid im Jahre 1919 ab: Ihre Lage war durch ihre innen- und außenpolitische Isolation unhaltbar geworden, auch wenn die politische Verantwortung der Verfassung nach bei den Regierungsmitgliedern lag.

were to take the utmost care to preserve and respect the impartiality of their office. This great ability to adapt to an increasingly democratic society in Luxembourg developed under Grand Duchess Charlotte and Grand Duke Jean into an outstanding characteristic of the dynasty. ◆ With rebellion brewing, Marie-Adélaïde abdicated in 1919; her isolation at home and abroad had made her position untenable, even though under the constitution political responsibility lay with the members of the Government.

■ La grande-duchesse Marie-Anne avec les princesses Marie-Adélaïde, Charlotte, Hilda, Antonie, Elisabeth et Sophie
■ Großherzogin Maria-Anna mit den Prinzessinnen Marie-Adelheid, Charlotte, Hilda, Antonia, Elisabeth und Sophie
■ Grand Duchess Maria-Anna with Princesses Marie-Adélaïde, Charlotte, Hilda, Antonia, Elisabeth and Sophie

La grande-duchesse Charlotte (1919-1964)

En janvier 1919, Charlotte (*1896 †1985), deuxième fille du grand-duc Guillaume IV et de la grande-duchesse Marie-Anne, succède à sa soeur aînée sur le trône grand-ducal. En novembre de la même année, elle épouse Félix de Bourbon, prince de Parme(*1893 †1970); six enfants naîtront de cette union. ◆ Les quarante cinq ans de règne de Charlotte correspondent à une étape capitale de l'histoire aujourd'hui plus que centenaire de la dynastie car ils contribuèrent à ancrer profondément dans la conscience populaire la signification de l'institution

La grande-duchesse Charlotte avec ses enfants dans le parc du château de Colmar-Berg

Großherzogin Charlotte mit ihren Kindern im Park des Schlosses von Colmar-Berg

Grand Duchess Charlotte with her children in the grounds of the Château de Colmar-Berg

Großherzogin Charlotte (1919-1964)

Im Januar 1919 folgte Charlotte (*1896 †1985), die zweite Tochter von Großherzog Wilhelm IV. und Großherzogin Maria-Anna, ihrer älteren Schwester auf den Thron. Im November des gleichen Jahres heiratete sie Félix von Bourbon, Prinz von Parma (*1893 †1970); aus dieser Ehe gingen sechs Kinder hervor. ◆ Ihre 45jährige Amtszeit charakterisiert eine entscheidende Etappe in der heute über 100jährigen Dynastiegeschichte, in der sich die Bedeutung dieser Institution für Luxemburg tief im Bewußtsein der Bevölkerung verankern konnte. ◆ Der Ausgangspunkt für diese Entwicklung war das Referendum von 1919, während das hohe Ansehen und die große Popularität der Monarchie sich zu einem großen Teil aus der bedeutenden Rolle der großherzoglichen Familie und insbesondere der Großherzogin Charlotte im Zweiten Weltkrieg erklären. Damals setzte sich die im Exil lebende Großherzogin im alliierten Lager dafür ein, daß das besetzte Luxemburg als unabhängiger Staat weiterbestehen und seine Eigenständigkeit international anerkannt werden müßte. Neben der Widerstandsbewegung der luxemburgischen Bevölkerung und seiner Regierung hat der entscheidende Einsatz der Großher-

Grand Duchess Charlotte (1919-1964)

In January 1919, Charlotte (b.1896, d.1985), the second daughter of Grand Duke William IV and Grand Duchess Maria-Anna, succeeded her elder sister. In November of the same year she married Félix of Bourbon, Prince of Parma (b.1893, d.1970); the marriage produced six children. ◆ The 45 years of Charlotte's reign were a crucial period in the history of the dynasty, which has now lasted for over 100 years; it was during her reign that the importance of the institution to Luxembourg became deeply rooted in the minds of the population. ◆ The high regard and great popularity enjoyed by the monarchy today are largely due to the important role played by the grand-ducal family, and especially Grand Duchess Charlotte, during the Second World War. During the war the Grand Duchess, who was living in exile, championed the cause of the independence of occupied Luxembourg within the Allied camp and pressed for international recognition of its autonomy. Alongside the resistance movement within the population and its Government, the vital commitment of the Grand Duchess helped to secure the present status of Luxembourg as a fully sovereign State in its own right. Through the complete identification

Les fiançailles
de la grande-duchesse
Charlotte avec
le prince Félix
de Bourbon-Parme,
le 5 octobre 1918

Verlobung von
Großherzogin
Charlotte mit
Prinz Felix von
Bourbon-Parma
am 5. Oktober 1918

Betrothal of
Grand Duchess
Charlotte
to Prince Félix
of Bourbon-Parma,
5 October 1918

monarchique pour le Luxembourg.
◆ L'origine de cette évolution se
trouve dans le référendum de 1919,
mais le grand prestige et l'immense
popularité de la monarchie s'expliquent surtout par le rôle prépondérant de la famille grand-ducale en
général et de la grande-duchesse
Charlotte en particulier durant la
Seconde Guerre mondiale. La
grande-duchesse alors exilée dans
le camp allié mettra tout en œuvre
pour que le Luxembourg occupé
continue d'exister en tant qu'État
indépendant et pour que son auto-
nomie soit reconnue sur la scène internationale. À côté du mouvement
de résistance de la population et du
gouvernement du pays, l'engagement décisif de la grande-duchesse
a contribué à assurer au Luxembourg le statut d'état à part entière et
émancipé dont il jouit aujourd'hui.
Grâce à une famille grand-ducale
qui s'identifiait complètement aux
intérêts du pays et qui défendait activement la souveraineté nationale
et grâce, de surcroît, à la personnalité impressionnante de la grande-
duchesse Charlotte, qui fut le premier chef d'État à parler le luxembourgeois, la dynastie désormais
luxembourgeoise allait devenir un
facteur d'intégration essentiel.

zogin zu dem gegenwärtigen Status
Luxemburgs als vollwertiger und
gleichberechtigter Staat beigetragen. Durch die vollkommene Identifikation der großherzoglichen Familie mit den Interessen Luxemburgs,
durch ihre aktive Verteidigung der
staatlichen Unabhängigkeit und
nicht zuletzt durch die beeindruk-
kende Persönlichkeit der Großherzogin Charlotte, die als erstes
Staatsoberhaupt Luxemburgisch
sprach, wurde die nunmehr luxemburgische Dynastie zu einem we-
sentlichen Integrationsfaktor.

of the grand ducal family with the
interests of Luxembourg, through
their active defence of its national
independence, and not least through
the engaging personality of Grand
Duchess Charlotte, the first Head of
State to speak the Luxembourgian
language, the House of Luxembourg,
as it was now known, became a major integrating factor.

▦ Le grand-duc Jean (depuis 1964)

Jean (*1921), fils aîné de la grande-duchesse Charlotte et du prince Félix de Bourbon-Parme, est grand-duc du Luxembourg depuis 1964. Il avait déjà défendu dignement les intérêts du pays avant de monter sur le trône, notamment durant les années de guerre lorsque, à l'instar de son père, il s'engagea volontairement dans les armées alliées. En 1953, il

▦ Großherzog Jean (seit 1964)

Seit 1964 ist Jean (*1921), der älteste Sohn von Großherzogin Charlotte und von Prinz Félix von Bourbon-Parma, Großherzog von Luxemburg. Vor seiner Thronbesteigung hatte er die Interessen des Landes bereits würdevoll verteidigt, besonders in den Kriegsjahren, als er gemeinsam mit seinem Vater Félix freiwillig in die Armeen der Alliier-

■ Grand Duke Jean (since 1964)

Since 1964, Jean (born 1921), the eldest son of Grand Duchess Charlotte and Prince Félix of Bourbon-Parma, has been the Grand Duke of Luxembourg. Before ascending the throne, he had already defended his country's interests with distinction, especially during the war years, when he volunteered for service in the Allied armies along with his fa-

▦ Le prince héritier Jean avec ses frère et soeurs les princesses Elisabeth, Marie-Adélaïde, Marie-Gabrielle, Alix et le prince Charles

▦ Erbprinz Jean mit seinen Schwestern, den Prinzessinnen Elisabeth, Marie-Adélaïde, Marie-Gabrielle und Alix und seinem Bruder, Prinz Charles

■ Jean, as Heir Apparent, with his sisters, the Princesses Elisabeth, Marie-Adélaïde, Marie-Gabrielle and Alix and his brother, Prince Charles

ten eingetreten war. Im Jahre 1953 hatte er Prinzessin Joséphine-Charlotte von Belgien geheiratet; aus ihrer Ehe gingen fünf Kinder hervor, darunter auch der jetzige Erbgroßherzog Henri.　Unter Großherzog Jean und seiner Familie hat sich die Beliebtheit der Dynastie weiter festigen können und heute, im Rahmen unseres schnellebigen Zeitalters, ist sie durch ihre vorbildhafte Rolle zu einem Symbol für Wert- und Traditionsbewußtsein geworden.　Am Ende des 20. Jahrhunderts versteht sich Großherzog Jean als ein modernes Staatsoberhaupt, das seine zahlreichen Funktionen wie Staatsbesuche oder Audienzen für Regierungsmitglieder, ausländische Staatsgäste, Diplomaten sowie

ther Félix. In 1953 he married Princess Joséphine-Charlotte of Belgium; their marriage has produced five children, including the present Heir Apparent Henri. ◆ Under Grand Duke Jean and his family the popularity of the dynasty has been further cemented, and today, in our rapidly changing world, their exemplary role reflects the values and traditions they cherish. ◆ As the 20th century draws to a close, Grand Duke Jean sees himself as a modern Head of State, undertaking numerous tasks such as state visits or audiences with cabinet ministers, foreign guests, diplomats and personalities from the political, sporting and cultural spheres in the interests of the country and its people. His in-

■ Le prince héritier Jean et les princesses Elisabeth et Marie-Adélaïde

■ Erbprinz Jean mit den Prinzessinnen Elisabeth und Marie-Adélaïde

■ Heir Apparent Prince Jean and the Princesses Elisabeth and Marie-Adélaïde

avait épousé la princesse Joséphine-Charlotte de Belgique; elle lui donna cinq enfants, parmi lesquels le grand-duc héritier actuel, Henri. ◆ Le grand-duc Jean et sa famille sont parvenus à accentuer encore la popularité d'une dynastie qui, dans l'époque agitée que nous traversons, est devenue, de par son rôle exemplaire, un symbole du sens des valeurs et de la tradition.

En cette fin de XXe siècle, le grand-duc Jean apparaît comme un chef d'État moderne qui assume ses multiples tâches (visites officielles ou audiences avec les membres du gouvernement, les invités officiels

étrangers, les diplomates et les personnalités du monde politique, sportif et culturel) dans l'intérêt du pays et de sa population. Sa participation à la vie quotidienne des Luxembourgeois se reflète particulièrement dans le choix des thèmes de ses messages de Noël annuels, ainsi que dans ses nombreuses visites d'institutions publiques, privées et sociales qui le conduisent, lui et sa famille, dans tous les cantons du pays.

Persönlichkeiten aus Politik, Sport und Kultur im Interesse des Landes und seiner Bevölkerung wahrnimmt. Seine Anteilnahme am Alltag der Luxemburger zeigt sich insbesondere bei der Themenauswahl der jährlichen Weihnachtsansprache wie auch bei den zahlreichen Besichtigungen in öffentlichen, privaten und sozialen Einrichtungen, die ihn und andere Mitglieder seiner Familie in sämtliche Kantone des Landes führen.

terest in the everyday life of Luxembourgers is especially evident in the choice of subjects for his annual Christmas address to the nation as well as in the numerous visits to public and private social institutions which take him and other members of his family into every canton of the country.

Henri: une enfance et une jeunesse exemplaires

e prince Henri, fils aîné de Jean et de Joséphine-Charlotte, la sœur des rois des Belges Baudoin Ier et Albert II, alors respectivement grand-duc et grande-duchesse héritiers, est né le 16 avril 1955. Avec ses frères et sœurs, la fille aînée Marie-Astrid, les jumeaux Jean et Margaretha et le fils Guillaume, il est élevé au manoir de Betzdorf, près de Grevenmacher. Après l'avènement de son père, la famille grand-ducale s'installe au château de Berg. C'est dans ce milieu transparent et très protégé qu'il passe une enfance insouciante et sans histoire, voire un peu recluse, où ses principaux repères sont non seulement ses grands-parents et ses parents, mais aussi ses frères et sœurs. Comme de coutume au Luxembourg, son éducation est axée sur les valeurs sociales-chrétiennes et c'est d'ailleurs ce cadre de référence qui imprégnera sa per-

Henri: Eine unbeschwerte Kindheit und Jugend

rinz Henri wurde am 16. April 1955 als ältester Sohn des damaligen Erbgroßherzogs Jean und der Erbgroßherzogin Joséphine-Charlotte, Schwester der belgischen Könige Baudouin und Albert, geboren. Er ist mit seinen vier Geschwistern, der älteren Schwester Marie-Astrid, den Zwillingen Jean und Margaretha und dem Bruder Guillaume auf dem Landsitz von Betzdorf in der Nähe von Grevenmacher aufgewachsen. Nach der Thronbesteigung seines Vaters lebte die großherzogliche Familie auf Schloß Berg. In dieser überschaubaren und sehr geschützten Umgebung verbrachte er eine sorgenfreie und einfache, wenn auch eine etwas abgeschirmte Kindheit, deren wichtigster Bezugspunkt neben den Großeltern und Eltern die Geschwister waren. Seine Erziehung orientierte sich - wie in Luxemburg üblich - an den Werten der

Henri: a carefree childhood and youth

rince Henri was born April 16, 1955 as the eldest son of Jean, who at that time was the Heir Apparent, and Joséphine-Charlotte, sister of the Belgian Kings Baudouin and Albert. He grew up in the country residence of Betzdorf, near Grevenmacher, with his two brothers and two sisters – his elder sister Marie-Astrid, the twins Jean and Margaretha and his brother Guillaume. After his father ascended the throne, the grand-ducal family lived in the Château de Berg. In this ordered and highly protected environment he spent a carefree and simple, if somewhat sheltered childhood, the main focal point, besides his parents and grandparents, being his brothers and sisters. His upbringing, as is customary in Luxembourg, was based on the values of Christian social teaching, and these values have continued to have a decisive influence on his personality to

sonnalité de façon décisive jusqu'à aujourd'hui. ◆ À l'âge de six ans, l'éducation du jeune prince est confiée à un précepteur qui lui donne d'abord des leçons privées en compagnie de quatre autres enfants, puis qui l'instruira seul au château de Berg. Le programme correspondait sensiblement aux matières officielles enseignées dans les écoles primaires luxembourgeoises et devait préparer l'écolier au lycée. Vers l'âge de douze ans, le prince Henri suit également certains cours au lycée classique de Diekirch. Cet enseignement fondamental fut complété par une formation pratique basée sur des visites d'expositions et d'ateliers d'art artisanal et des excursions dans la nature ou dans des villes d'intérêt historique. L'élève Henri, sollicité par ses nombreux devoirs et obligations officiels, était particulièrement féru de géographie, d'histoire du Luxembourg et de sciences sociales. Son intérêt profond envers l'évolution sociale et culturelle se reflète aujourd'hui encore dans sa fascination pour les civilisations et les mœurs étrangères, spécialement la culture asiatique. Dans le domaine artistique et littéraire, le jeune prince éprouva très tôt une affinité particulière pour la grande musique et il l'entretient encore maintenant en assistant fréquemment à des concerts classiques. Les jours ou les après-midi

christlichen Soziallehre, und es ist auch dieser Wertbezug, der seine Persönlichkeit bis heute entscheidend prägt. Im Alter von sechs Jahren wurde die Ausbildung des jungen Prinzen einem Hauslehrer anvertraut, der ihn zuerst mit vier anderen Kindern privat unterrichtete und der ihn danach allein auf Schloß Berg betreute. Das Programm entsprach weitgehend den offiziellen Fächern in den luxemburgischen Primärschulen; es sollte den Schüler auf den Lyzeumsabschluß vorbereiten. Mit etwa zwölf Jahren belegte Prinz Henri ebenfalls einige Kurse im klassischen Lyzeum von Diekirch. Diese Grundausbildung wurde ergänzt durch konkreten Anschauungsunterricht wie die Besichtigung von Ausstellungen, den Besuch von Kunsthandwerksstätten oder auch durch Ausflüge in die Natur und in historisch sehenswerte Städte. Der von vielfältigen Aufgaben und offiziellen Verpflichtungen beanspruchte Schüler zeigte sich besonders beeindruckt von der Geographie, der Geschichte Luxemburgs und den Sozialwissenschaften. Sein tiefgehendes Interesse für gesellschaftliche und kulturelle Entwicklungen zeigt sich noch heute in seiner Faszination für fremde Zivilisationen und Lebensweisen wie vor allem hinsichtlich der asiatischen Kultur. Im schöngeistigen Bereich entwickelte der junge

the present day. ◆ When he was six years old, the task of educating the young prince was entrusted to a tutor, who initially gave him private lessons along with four other children and subsequently gave him individual tuition in the Château de Berg. The subjects taught largely corresponded to the official curriculum of primary schools in Luxembourg, and the teaching programme was designed to prepare the pupil for entry into a senior secondary school (lycée). At the age of about twelve Prince Henri also attended some classes in the grammar school in Diekirch. This grounding was supplemented by visual instruction, including visits to exhibitions and craft studios as well as outings to the country for nature study and to towns of historical interest. The prince, who was called upon to fulfil a wide range of responsibilities and official engagements, found geography, the history of Luxembourg and the social sciences especially stimulating. His profound interest in social and cultural developments is still visible today in the fascination that foreign cultures and ways of life hold for him, especially the culture of Asia. In the artistic domain the prince developed a special affinity for classical music from a very early age; this is reflected today in his regular attendance at classical concerts. On the days and after-

de congé, Henri, passionné par les animaux et par la nature, pratiquait l'équitation, la pêche, la natation, le ski et la randonnée. Pendant les vacances scolaires, ses lieux de villégiature préférés étaient la côte belge, la Côte d'Azur et les Alpes suisses pour la pratique du ski. ◆ Non content de remplir ses obligations scolaires, le jeune prince participera régulièrement à des cérémonies officielles dès son enfance. Invité de marque toujours très apprécié, il soulignait par sa présence l'importance de ces manifestations. Sa carrière en tant que fils aîné et successeur de son père était donc toute tracée depuis son plus jeune âge et en même temps marquée par des devoirs et des règles protocolaires qui limitaient étroitement sa liberté individuelle et son libre arbitre. Sa préparation aux tâches qui l'attendaient et qui demandaient un sens des responsabilités, une discrétion et une force de caractère considérables, une excellente formation et des connaissances générales étendues s'effectua essentiellement grâce à l'expérience de son entourage immédiat. Outre ses parents, sa grand-mère, la grande-duchesse Charlotte, avec sa forte personnalité et sa nature pétrie d'humour, joua un rôle prépondérant dans l'évolution du jeune prince. ◆ La première phase de sa scolarité au château de Berg prit fin à l'âge de

Prinz sehr früh eine besondere Affinität zur klassischen Musik, die noch heute im regelmäßigen Besuch von klassischen Konzerten zum Ausdruck kommt. An den schulfreien Tagen und Nachmittagen widmete sich der tierliebende und naturverbundene Prinz dem Reiten, Fischen, Schwimmen, Skifahren und der Pfadfinderbewegung. In den Schulferien waren die belgische Küste, die Côte d'Azur und die Schweizer Alpen zum Skifahren beliebte Reiseziele. Neben den schulischen Pflichten nahm der junge Prinz bereits seit seiner Kindheit regelmäßig an öffentlichen Veranstaltungen teil. Immer war er ein gern gesehener hoher Gast, der die Bedeutung dieser Anlässe unterstrich. So war sein Lebensweg als erstgeborener Sohn und Nachfolger seines Vaters seit seiner frühesten Kindheit vorgezeichnet und gleichzeitig geprägt durch protokollarische Vorgaben und Regeln - eine Tatsache, die seine persönlichen Freiheiten und Wahlmöglichkeiten eng eingrenzte. Auf seine späteren Aufgaben, die ein großes Verantwortungsgefühl, Diskretion, Charakterstärke, eine gute Bildung sowie ein fundamentales Allgemeinwissen erfordern, wurde er hauptsächlich durch die Erfahrungen seiner engsten Umgebung vorbereitet. Neben den Eltern ist es die Großmutter, Großherzogin Charlotte, die mit ihrer Persönlich-

noons when there was no school, the Prince, with his great love of animals and the natural world, devoted himself to riding, fishing, swimming, skiing and scouting. During the school holidays the Belgian coast, the French Riviera and the ski resorts of the Swiss Alps were popular destinations. ◆ Alongside his schooling, the young prince regularly took part from early childhood in public engagements. He was always welcome as a guest of honour, his presence underlining the importance of special events. This was the path marked out for him as his father's eldest son and heir from his earliest childhood, a path marked by the rules and formalities of protocol; this severely restricted his personal freedom and options. The main source of preparation for his subsequent duties, which would require a strong sense of responsibility, discretion, strength of character, a good education and a wealth of basic general knowledge, was his experience of those closest to him. Besides his parents, his grandmother, Grand Duchess Charlotte, with her strong personality and keen sense of humour, played an important part in the development of the young prince. ◆ At the age of 14 Prince Henri completed his initial schooling in the Château de Berg. Like many young people of his age, the prince went to a senior secondary

quatorze ans. Henri fréquenta ensuite, comme beaucoup de jeunes de son âge, un lycée à Nice où il obtint son baccalauréat. En 1975, il réussit l'examen de sortie de la fameuse Académie royale militaire de Sandhurst, qu'il quitta avec le grade de lieutenant. Il occupe actuellement le rang de colonel au sein de l'armée luxembourgeoise. ◆ La personnalité noble et équilibrée du grand-duc héritier se caractérise par la retenue et la discrétion. Son rayonnement serein procure une impression de correction et de distinction. Il traite son entourage immédiat avec un esprit d'ouverture et une capacité de tolérance remarquables. Il attache beaucoup de prix à la protection de sa vie privée. Ses traits les plus marquants sont une conception simple de la vie, une connaissance étonnante des hommes, une grande capacité de réflexion et un sens aigu de la famille. Depuis sa prime enfance, il entretient une relation très étroite avec sa patrie et avec son environnement naturel, qui représente pour lui un dérivatif irremplaçable à ses tâches officielles. Ses nombreuses visites dans les différentes contrées du pays et ses contacts très proches avec les Luxembourgeois l'ont profondément uni à la population autochtone. En tant qu'Européen, il considère l'intégration européenne comme une évolution naturelle et indispensable

keit und ihrer humorvollen Art eine wichtige Rolle in der Entwicklung des jungen Prinzen spielte. ◆ Im Alter von 14 Jahren endeten die frühen Lehrjahre auf Schloß Berg. Danach besuchte der junge Prinz wie viele gleichaltrige Jugendliche ein Lyzeum in Nizza, wo er das Abitur ablegte. Im Jahre 1975 absolvierte er die renommierte königliche Militärakademie von Sandhurst, die er als Leutnant abschloß. ◆ Die vornehme und ausgeglichene Persönlichkeit des Erbgroßherzogs charakterisiert sich durch Zurückhaltung und Diskretion. Seine selbstbeherrschte Ausstrahlung vermittelt den Eindruck von Korrektheit und Stilgefühl. Seiner nächsten Umgebung begegnet er mit einer auffallenden Offenheit und der Fähigkeit zur Toleranz. Er legt besonderen Wert auf die Wahrung seines Privatlebens; zu seinen herausragenden Eigenschaften gehören eine unkomplizierte Lebenseinstellung, eine bemerkenswerte Menschenkenntnis, die Fähigkeit zur Reflexion und ein ausgeprägter Familiensinn. Seit seiner frühen Kindheit pflegte er eine sehr enge Beziehung zu seiner Heimat und zu der ihn umgebenden Natur, die für ihn einen wichtigen Ausgleich zu seinen offiziellen Aufgaben darstellt. Durch seine zahlreichen Besuche in den verschiede-

school in Nice, where he passed his baccalauréat six years later. In 1975 he underwent officer training at the renowned Royal Military Academy of Sandhurst, passing out as a lieutenant. In the Luxembourg army today he holds the rank of colonel. ◆ The refined and well-balanced personality of the Heir Apparent is expressed in his reserve and discretion. The composure he radiates conveys a sense of propriety and decorum. Those he meets cannot fail to observe his openness and capacity for tolerance. He attaches special importance to the preservation of his private life; among his outstanding qualities are an uncomplicated attitude to life, a remarkable knowledge of human nature, a capacity for logical reflection and a pronounced sense of family. Since early childhood he has nurtured very close links with his home area and its natural surroundings, which serve as an important counterweight to his official duties. His numerous visits to the various parts of the country and his close contact with Luxembourgers have made him very attached to the local people. As a European he regards the move towards ever closer European integration in the wake of the horrors of World War II as a natural and necessary development, especially in terms of its importance to Luxembourg. ◆ Among his preferred leisure activi-

eu égard aux événements de la Seconde Guerre mondiale, surtout compte tenu de la signification de ce processus pour le Luxembourg. ◆ Ses passe-temps favoris sont notamment la musique classique, le ski, le tennis, la natation, la chasse, la littérature et l'escrime.

nen Gegenden des Landes und seinen engen Kontakt zu den Luxemburgern ist er der einheimischen Bevölkerung sehr verbunden. Als Europäer empfindet er die zunehmende europäische Integration vor dem Hintergrund der Ereignisse des Zweiten Weltkrieges als eine natürliche und notwendige Entwicklung, insbesondere hinsichtlich deren Bedeutung für Luxemburg. ◆ Zu seinen bevorzugten Freizeitbeschäftigungen gehören die klassische Musik, das Skifahren, das Tennis, das Schwimmen, die Jagd, die Literatur, das Fechten.

ties are classical music, skiing, tennis, swimming, hunting, literature and swordfencing.

■ Le prince Henri avec ses parents, le grand-duc héritier Jean et la grande-duchesse héritière Joséphine-Charlotte, ainsi que ses grands-parents, la grande-duchesse Charlotte et le prince Félix

▨ Prinz Henri mit seinen Eltern, Erbgroßherzog Jean und Erbgroßherzogin Joséphine-Charlotte, und seinen Großeltern, Großherzogin Charlotte und Prinz Felix

■ Prince Henri with his parents, Heir Apparent Prince Jean and Princess Joséphine-Charlotte and his grandparents, Grand Duchess Charlotte and Prince Félix

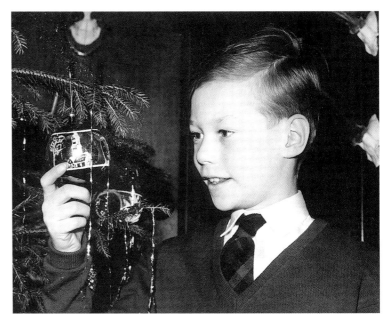

■ L'enfance du prince Henri dans le cadre familial du château de Betzdorf

■ Prinz Henris Kindheit im familiären Rahmen des Betzdorfer Schlosses

■ Family scenes from the childhood of Prince Henri at the Château de Betzdorf

La vie familiale au château de Betzdorf.
Sur la photo du bas, on reconnaît, de gauche à
droite, les princesses Marie-Astrid et Margaretha
et les princes Guillaume, Jean et Henri
avec leurs parents.

Familienleben im Schloß von Betzdorf.
Auf dem unteren Foto von links nach rechts:
die Prinzessinnen Marie-Astrid und Margaretha sowie die Prinzen Guillaume, Jean und Henri
mit ihren Eltern.

Family life at the Château de Betzdorf.
The bottom photograph shows, from left to right,
Princesses Marie-Astrid and Margaretha
and Princes Guillaume, Henri and Jean
with their parents.

Première communion du prince Henri et de la princesse Marie-Astrid au château de Betzdorf en 1962. Outre leurs parents assistent également le prince Jean et la princesse Margaretha, le roi Baudouin et la reine Fabiola, la grande-duchesse Charlotte ainsi que la princesse Marie-Gabrielle de Luxembourg.

Prinz Henri und Prinzessin Marie-Astrid bei ihrer Erstkommunion im Schloß von Betzdorf im Jahr 1962. Neben den Eltern wohnen auch Prinz Jean und Prinzessin Margaretha, König Baudouin und Königin Fabiola, Großherzogin Charlotte und Prinzessin Marie-Gabrielle von Luxemburg dem Ereignis bei.

First Communion of Prince Henri and Princess Marie-Astrid at the Château de Betzdorf in 1962. Besides their parents, the photograph also shows Prince Jean and Princess Margaretha, King Baudouin and Queen Fabiola, Grand Duchess Charlotte and Princess Marie-Gabrielle of Luxembourg.

■ L'éducation d'un jeune prince. Le cours de gymnastique où l'on reconnaît, de droite à gauche, les princes Henri et Jean ainsi que les princesses Marie-Astrid et Margaretha.
page de droite: La salle de classe au palais grand-ducal en 1963 où le prince Henri suit les cours de M. Aloyse Raths en compagnie de la princesse Marie-Astrid

Erziehung eines jungen Prinzen: die Prinzen Henri und Jean sowie die Prinzessinnen Marie-Astrid und Margaretha beim Turnunterricht (von rechts nach links).
Rechte Seite: Der Klassensaal des großherzoglichen Palasts im Jahr 1963, wo Prinz Henri und Prinzessin Marie-Astrid von ihrem Lehrer Aloyse Raths unterrichtet werden.

■ Education of a young prince. Gymnastic lesson with, from right to left, the Princes Henri and Jean and the Princesses Marie-Astrid and Margaretha.
Right: the classroom in the grand-ducal palace in 1963, where Prince Henri and Princess Marie-Astrid are being taught by their tutor, Mr Aloyse Raths.

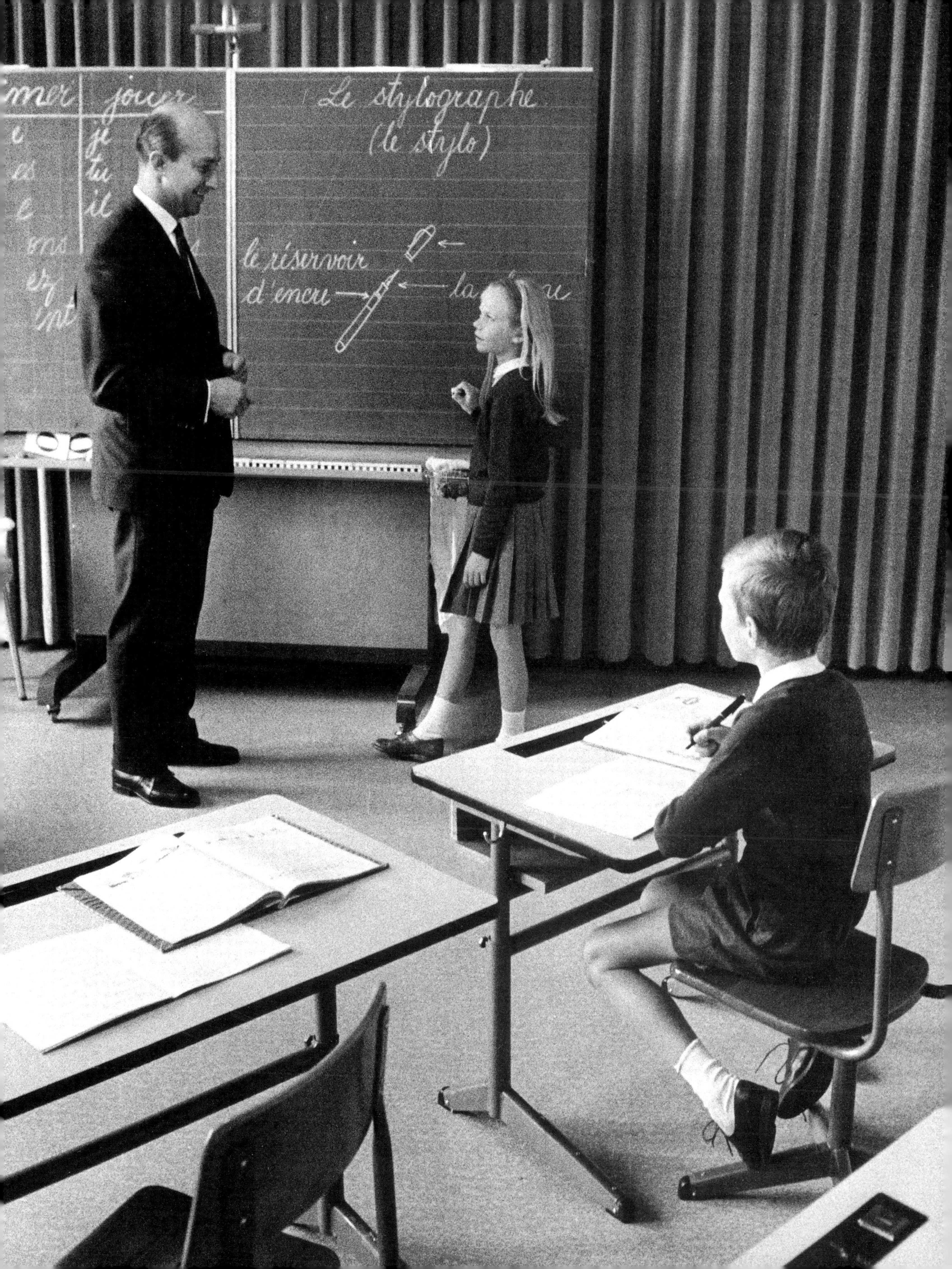
Le stylographe
(le stylo)
jouer
le réservoir
d'encre

Les années d'adolescence:
vie familiale, détente et sorties officielles

Das Jugendalter:
Familienleben, Freizeit und offizielle Auftritte

The adolescent years:
family life, relaxation and official engagements

Maria Teresa: une enfance et une jeunesse pleines de variété

Maria Teresa Mestre, fille aînée d'une famille de banquiers catholiques de La Havane, est née le 22 mars 1956. Son père, José Antonio Mestre, et sa mère, Maria Teresa Batista-Falla de Mestre, sont issus tous les deux de familles bourgeoises espagnoles aisées. Jusqu'à l'âge de neuf ans et l'installation définitive de sa famille à Genève, Maria Teresa a vécu son enfance avec son frère aîné Antonio et ses frère et sœur cadets Luis et Catalina à La Havane puis à New York. Afin de ne pas perdre définitivement le contact avec l'Espagne, les Mestre passaient toutes les vacances scolaires dans leur propriété familiale de Santander, sur la côte cantabrique. La révolution cubaine ayant éclaté, ils se fixent à New York où Maria Teresa fréquente l'école primaire américaine de Marymount, puis l'École française. La jeune fille poursuit ses études dans l'enseigne-

Maria Teresa: Eine abwechslungs- reiche Kindheit und Jugend

Maria Teresa Mestre wurde am 22. März 1956 als älteste Tochter einer katholischen Bankiersfamilie in Havanna geboren. Ihr Vater, José Antonio Mestre und ihre Mutter, Maria Teresa Batista-Falla de Mestre, stammen beide aus wohlhabenden spanischen Bürgerfamilien. Bis zu ihrem 9. Lebensjahr und der endgültigen Niederlassung der Familie in Genf verbrachte Maria Teresa ihre Kindheit zusammen mit ihrem älteren Bruder Antonio und ihren jüngeren Geschwistern Luis und Catalina in Havanna und danach in New York. Damit der Kontakt zu Spanien nicht ganz verlorenging, verbrachten die Mestre jede Schulferien auf ihrem Familienbesitz in Santander, an der Atlantikküste Spaniens. Nach dem Ausbruch der kubanischen Revolution lebten die Eltern in New York, wo Maria Teresa die amerikanische Grundschule in

Maria Teresa: an eventful childhood and youth

Maria Teresa Mestre was born in Havana March 22, 1956, the eldest daughter in a Catholic banker's family. Her father, José Antonio Mestre, and her mother, Maria Teresa Batista-Falla de Mestre, both came from prosperous Spanish merchant families. Until her ninth year, when the family finally settled in Geneva, Maria Teresa spent her childhood with her elder brother Antonio and her younger brother and sister, Luis and Catalina, in Havana and New York. So as not to break their ties with Spain completely, the Mestre family spent all of the school holidays on their family estate in Santander, on the Spanish Atlantic coast. After the outbreak of the Cuban revolution in 1959, her parents moved to New York, where Maria Teresa visited the American elementary school in Marymount and later attended the French lycée. This edu-

ment français lorsque sa famille s'établit en Suisse. Elle étudie d'abord à l'école Marie-Josée, à Gstaad. Elle séjourne ensuite pendant plus de sept ans au pensionnat pour jeunes filles Marie-Thérèse, à Genève, qui se distingue de la plupart des établissements traditionnels par son multilinguisme, son environnement multiculturel et ses principes éducatifs fondés sur la tolérance et le respect mutuel. Elle y obtient son baccalauréat en lettres, philosophie et langues en 1975. ◆ Malgré son parcours quelque peu agité accompagné de nombreux changements de lieu, la jeune Maria Teresa a toujours conservé comme valeur de référence essentielle et prépondérante, la famille et son enracinement profond dans la tradition éducationnelle européenne. Cette identification intense avec le milieu familial en tant que valeur intrinsèque est capitale pour comprendre sa personnalité d'aujourd'hui. Son éducation sévère et protégée correspond parfaitement à la tradition latine qui veut que les enfants vivent sous le toit paternel jusqu'au mariage. Le but essentiel consistait à former une jeune femme de bonne éducation et cultivée qui atteindrait l'âge adulte aussi intacte que possible. Outre ses origines familiales et sa foi catholique, c'est surtout la mentalité cosmopolite et humaniste qui lui a été inculquée chez ses pa-

Marymount und später die französische Schule besuchte. Die Erziehung im französischen Bildungssystem wurde auch fortgesetzt, nachdem die Familie in der Schweiz lebte. Dort studierte sie zuerst an der Marie-Josée Schule in Gstaad und danach während mehr als sieben Jahren am Mädchenpensionnat Marie-Thérèse in Genf, das sich durch die Vielsprachigkeit, das multikulturelle Umfeld und das auf Toleranz und gegenseitigen Respekt aufbauende Erziehungskonzept von den meisten herkömmlichen Schulen unterscheidet. Dort legte sie im Jahre 1975 das französische Abitur in Literatur, Philosophie und Sprachen ab. ◆ Ungeachtet des abwechslungsreichen Lebenslaufes, der mit zahlreichen Ortswechseln verbunden war, blieb die Familie mit ihrer tiefen Verwurzelung in der europäischen Bildungstradition der wichtigste und prägendste Wertbezug im Leben der jungen Maria Teresa. Diese starke Identifikation mit der Familie als Wert an sich ist bis heute wesentlich für das Verständnis ihrer Persönlichkeit. Ihre strenge und wohlbehütete Erziehung entsprach ganz der lateinischen Tradition, nach der die Kinder bis zu ihrer Heirat im Elternhaus wohnen. Im Mittelpunkt stand die Heranbildung einer wohlerzogenen und gebildeten jungen Frau, die das Erwachsenenleben möglichst

cation under the French system was continued when the family moved to Switzerland, where Maria Teresa initially attended the Marie-Josée school in Gstaad, followed by over seven years at the Marie-Thérèse girls' boarding school in Geneva, a school that differed from most conventional schools in its multilingualism, its multicultural environment and its educational ethos based on tolerance and mutual respect. It was there, in 1975, that Maria Teresa took her French baccalauréat in literature, philosophy and languages. ◆ Despite the changes in her life, which resulted from moving home on numerous occasions, the family, with its deep roots in the European educational tradition, remained the most important and formative source of values in the life of young Maria Teresa. This strong identification with the family as a value per se remains the key to understanding her personality today. Her strict and sheltered upbringing was entirely in line with the Latin tradition whereby children lived in the parental home until their marriage. At the heart of this tradition was the development of a well-bred, educated young woman who was to reach adulthood in the most intact condition possible. Besides her family roots and Catholic faith, her thinking was also permanently influenced by the cosmopolitan and

rents et à l'école qui a constamment influencé sa pensée. Ainsi, l'écolière Maria Teresa, élevée dans un environnement résolument multinational, s'est distinguée très tôt par une ouverture d'esprit remarquable, un sens critique aigu et, dans l'ensemble, une personnalité affirmée. Sur le plan des relations interpersonnelles, ces traits de caractère transparaissent principalement dans son sens des responsabilités développé, son esprit de solidarité et sa facilité de communiquer. En outre, ce sont certainement aussi ces qualités qui expliquent, en grande partie, son action pour des problèmes humanitaires tels que la pauvreté, la faim et la misère, ainsi que son engagement professionnel ultérieur au service de la Croix Rouge internationale. Cet intérêt très prononcé pour les causes sociales, qui marquera sa vie et ses activités futures comme une espèce de leitmotiv, est nourri par une longue tradition familiale. Tant du côté de son père, chez les Mestre, que du côté de sa mère, chez les Batista-Falla, on soutenait généreusement les associations sociales et culturelles. Son grand-père, par exemple, a grandement contribué à la création de la Société philharmonique de Cuba; dans le domaine social, il a en outre œuvré au développement de l'infrastructure médicale en favorisant la construction de centres de

intakt erreichen sollte. Neben den familiären Wurzeln und dem katholischen Glauben ist es vor allem die im Elternhaus und in der Schule vermittelte weltoffene und humanistische Geisteshaltung, die ihr Denken nachhaltig beeinflußte. So charakterisierte sich die in einem betont multinationalen Umfeld aufgewachsene Schülerin Maria Teresa bereits sehr früh durch eine ausgesprochene geistige Offenheit, einen kritischen Sinn wie insgesamt durch eine starke und entschlossene Persönlichkeit. Im zwischenmenschlichen Bereich kommen diese Merkmale hauptsächlich in ihrem großen Verantwortungsbewußtsein, ihrem Solidaritätsgefühl und in ihrer Leichtigkeit in der Kommunikation zum Tragen. Und sicherlich sind es auch zu einem großen Teil diese Eigenschaften, die ihr aktives Interesse für humanitäre Themen wie Armut, Hunger oder Not erklären wie auch ihren späteren Berufswunsch, für das Internationale Rote Kreuz tätig werden zu wollen. Dieses stark ausgeprägte soziale Interesse, das ihren Lebensweg und ihre späteren Tätigkeitsfelder wie eine Art Leitmotiv bestimmen wird, wurde von einer langen Familientradition genährt. Sowohl väterlicherseits, bei den Mestre, als auch mütterlicherseits, bei den Batista-Falla, wurden soziale und kulturelle Einrichtungen großzügig unterstützt. So wirkte

humanist attitudes she acquired, especially in the parental home and at school. Growing up in this emphatically multinational environment, the schoolgirl Maria Teresa was quick to reveal an extremely receptive intellect, discerning judgement and generally great strength of character and determination. In her dealings with other people these qualities are primarily reflected in her keen sense of responsibility, her feeling of solidarity and her ease of communication. And these same qualities surely also go a long way to explaining her active interest in humanitarian problems such as poverty, famine and distress as well as her subsequent desire to work for the International Red Cross. This very pronounced interest in social matters, which was to determine the subsequent course of her life and the nature of her activities, recurring time and again like a leitmotiv, was nurtured by a long family tradition. Both the Mestre family on her father's side and the Batista–Falla family on her mother's side were used to giving generous support to social and cultural institutions. Her grandfather, for example, played a vital part in the establishment of the Philharmonic Society in Cuba. In the social domain he was also committed to the development of a system of general health care and advocated the construction of preventive care

médecine préventive. Cette tradition a été perpétuée par les parents. ◆ Pendant ses loisirs, la jeune fille s'adonnait à sa passion du ballet, qu'elle pratiqua plus de dix-sept années durant. ◆ La personnalité naturelle et ouverte de Maria Teresa se traduit par un rayonnement intense et une grande joie de vivre. Elle observe, vis-à-vis d'elle-même et de son entourage, une ligne de conduite très exigeante qui s'exprime parfaitement dans ses activités diversifiées, son bon goût et son sens profond des responsabilités à l'égard des problèmes de société. Sa maîtrise parfaite de l'espagnol, de l'anglais et du français et sa bonne connaissance du luxembourgeois, de l'allemand et de l'italien illustrent l'étendue de sa formation et son immense besoin d'épanouissement personnel. Ce multilinguisme est sans doute le meilleur reflet de ses véritables convictions européennes, qui sont profondément enracinées dans son parcours personnel. Les qualités essentielles de Maria Teresa sont notamment le dynamisme et l'engagement, l'esprit d'initiative, une intelligence intuitive et un sens extraordinairement développé de la famille. La princesse, qui s'intéresse beaucoup aux questions philosophiques, trouve son soutien spirituel dans la foi qu'elle vit comme une expérience quotidienne. Sa nature liante, son

ihr Großvater zum Beispiel entscheidend am Aufbau der philharmonischen Gesellschaft auf Kuba mit. Außerdem setzte er sich auf dem sozialen Gebiet für die Entwicklung der medizinischen Infrastruktur ein, indem er den Bau von Gesundheitsvorsorgestellen anregte. Diese Tradition wurde von ihren Eltern fortgesetzt. In der Freizeit galt Maria Teresas Leidenschaft dem Ballett, das sie während mehr als 17 Jahren tanzte. Maria Teresas natürliche und aufgeschlossene Persönlichkeit zeichnet sich durch eine starke Ausstrahlung und durch eine große Lebensfreude aus. Gegenüber sich selbst und ihrer Umgebung hegt sie eine sehr anspruchsvolle Lebenshaltung, die sehr gut in ihren vielseitigen Aktivitäten, ihrem guten Geschmack wie auch in ihrem ausgeprägten Verantwortungsgefühl gegenüber gesellschaftlichen und sozialen Themen zum Ausdruck kommt. Ihr perfektes Spanisch, Englisch, Französisch und ihre guten Kenntnisse in Luxemburgisch, Deutsch und Italienisch sind beispielhaft für ihre umfassende Bildung und ihr ausgeprägtes Bedürfnis nach persönlicher Weiterentwicklung. Diese Vielsprachigkeit spiegelt vielleicht am besten ihre wahrhaft europäische Gesinnung wider, die sehr tief in ihrem persönlichen Lebensweg verwurzelt ist. Zu ihren herausragenden Eigenschaf-

centres. This tradition was continued by Maria Teresa's parents. ◆ In her free time Maria Teresa's great passion was ballet, which she danced for over 17 years. ◆ Maria Teresa's natural demeanour and her open-mindedness make her a very charismatic and enthusiastic person. She makes very high demands of herself and her surroundings, a fact which is clearly expressed in her widely varied activities, her good taste and in the obvious sense of responsibility with which she addresses social issues. Her perfect Spanish, English and French, as well as her good knowledge of Luxembourgian, German and Italian, illustrate the breadth of her education and her pronounced desire to continue her personal development. Perhaps it is this multilingualism that best reflects her truly European sentiments, which are deeply rooted in her own history. Among her outstanding characteristics are dynamism and commitment, initiative, intuitive understanding and an extremely highly developed sense of family. Maria Teresa, who has a keen interest in philosophical questions, draws spiritual sustenance from her deep Catholic faith, which she regards as an intensive experience discovered afresh every day. Thanks to her sociability, her traditional upbringing and her strong need to put down roots, she

éducation traditionnelle et son grand besoin de racines ont très rapidement créé une affinité considérable entre elle et la population luxembourgeoise et avec le pays. Certainement depuis son mariage avec le grand-duc héritier Henri et ses nombreuses visites dans tous les coins du pays, cette relation très étroite et cordiale est devenue tout à fait réciproque, d'autant plus que la jeune princesse a entre-temps appris à parler couramment l'idiome du pays et peut donc s'entretenir avec les Luxembourgeois dans leur langue. ◆ Maria Teresa consacre ses loisirs à des activités très diversifiées comprenant le ski, la natation, le patinage, le ballet, la littérature, la décoration et le jardinage.

ten gehören ein dynamisches und engagiertes Wesen, Initiativfähigkeit, ein intuitiver Verstand wie ein außerordentlich entwickelter Familiensinn. Den geistigen Rückhalt findet die an philosophischen Fragen sehr interessierte Prinzessin im Glauben, der für sie eine täglich erlebte Erfahrung darstellt. Durch ihr kontaktfreudiges Wesen, ihre traditionelle Erziehung und ihr starkes Bedürfnis nach Verwurzelung konnte sie sehr schnell eine große Affinität zu der luxemburgischen Bevölkerung wie auch zu dem Land entwickeln. Spätestens seit ihrer Heirat mit Erbgroßherzog Henri und ihren zahlreichen Besuchen in allen Teilen des Landes ist diese sehr enge und herzliche Beziehung durchaus gegenseitig und dies um so mehr, als die junge Prinzessin inzwischen die luxemburgische Sprache fließend beherrscht und sich somit in der Landessprache mit den Luxemburgern unterhält. ◆ Die vielfältigen Freizeitbeschäftigungen von Maria Teresa umfassen das Skifahren, das Schwimmen, das Schlittschuhlaufen, das Ballett, die Literatur, die Innendekoration und die Gartenpflege.

was able to develop a strong affinity to the people of Luxembourg and their country within a very short time. Even before she married Prince Henri but certainly since then, through her numerous visits to all parts of the country, this very close and warm relationship has been entirely mutual, all the more so since the young princess now speaks the Luxembourgian language fluently and addresses Luxembourgers in their own tongue. ◆ Maria Teresa's diverse leisure pursuits include skiing, swimming, ice-skating, ballet, literature, interior decoration and gardening.

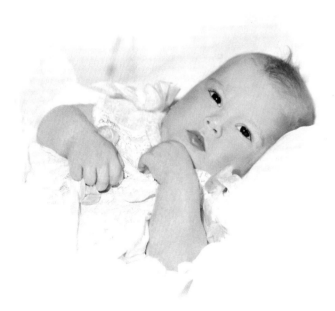

■ Maria Teresa a passé ses trois premières années dans cette belle demeure du quartier El Vedado à la Havane. On la voit ici avec sa mère, Mme Maria Teresa Batista-Falla de Mestre et son frère aîné Antonio.

■ In diesem wunderschönen Anwesen in El Vedado, einem Stadtviertel von Havanna, verbrachte Maria Teresa ihre ersten drei Lebensjahre. Hier mit ihrer Mutter, Maria Teresa Batista-Falla de Mestre, und ihrem älteren Bruder Antonio.

■ Maria Teresa spent the first three years of her life in this beautiful villa in the El Vedado suburb of Havana. Here we see her with her mother, Maria Teresa Batista-Falla de Mestre, and her elder brother Antonio.

■ Maria Teresa à Varadero (Cuba) avec son père,
M. José Antonio Mestre, et son frère Antonio

▨ Maria Teresa mit ihrem Vater, José Antonio Mestre,
und ihrem Bruder Antonio in Varadero (Kuba)

■ Maria Teresa in Varadero (Cuba) with her father,
José Antonio Mestre, and her brother Antonio

■ *Page de droite:* La Havane 1957

▨ *Rechte Seite:* Havanna 1957

■ *Right page:* Havana 1957

Les voyages des années d'enfance.

Comme tous les ans, Maria Teresa passe ses vacances d'été dans la propriété familiale de Santander en Espagne. On la voit ici avec sa grand-mère maternelle Mme Maria Teresa Falla-Bonet, en août 1962.

Au Central Park de New York avec sa soeur Catalina en 1963.

Dans l'appartement familial de Park Avenue avec sa soeur Catalina et ses frères Antonio et Luis en 1965.

Reisen in der Kindheit.

Die Sommerferien verbringt Maria Teresa jedes Jahr auf dem Familienanwesen von Santander in Spanien. Hier mit ihrer Großmutter mütterlicherseits, Maria Teresa Falla-Bonet, im August 1962.

Maria Teresa mit ihrer Schwester Catalina 1963 im New Yorker Central Park.

Mit ihrer Schwester Catalina und den Brüdern Antonio und Luis 1965 im Appartement der Familie in der Park Avenue.

Childhood holidays.

Every year Maria Teresa's summer holidays were spent on the family estate by Santander in Spain. Here we see her with her grandmother, Maria Teresa Falla-Bonet, in August 1962.

In Central Park, New York, with her sister Catalina in 1963.

In the family apartment on Park Avenue with her sister Catalina and her brothers Antonio and Luis in 1965.

Page de gauche:
De la promenade à Varadero (Cuba) en 1959 aux sports d'hiver à Saint-Moritz en 1958
De 1959 à 1965, la famille s'installe à New York
Maria Teresa à Central Park

Linke Seite:

Von der Promenade in Varadero (Kuba) im Jahr 1959 bis zum Wintersport in St. Moritz 1958
Von 1959 bis 1965 wohnte die Familie in New York
Maria Teresa im Central Park

Left page:
Walking in Varadero (Cuba) in 1959; winter sports in Saint-Moritz in 1958
From 1959 to 1965, the family lived in New York
Maria Teresa in Central Park

La famille s'installe
à Genève en 1965.
Sur la photo du bas,
on reconnaît, de gauche à
droite: Maria Teresa,
Catalina, Antonio,
M. et Mme Mestre et Luis
devant un portrait du
grand-père maternel,
M. Agustin Batista y
Gonzalez de Mendoza

1965 läßt sich die Familie
in Genf nieder.
Auf dem unteren Foto von
links nach rechts:
Maria Teresa, Catalina,
Antonio, Herr und Frau
Mestre und Luis vor einem
Porträt des Großvaters
mütterlicherseits, Agustin
Batista y Gonzalez de
Mendoza

The family moved
to Geneva in 1965.
In the bottom photograph,
from left to right, are Maria
Teresa, Catalina, Antonio,
Sr and Sra Mestre and Luis
in front of a portrait of the
children's maternal
grandfather, Agustin Batista
y Gonzalez de Mendoza.

gauche/links/left:
New York, 1965

Les études communes à Genève

e grand-duc héritier Henri et Maria Teresa se sont connus en 1975 au début de leurs études à Genève, une ville qui, avec son mélange fascinant de fonctionnaires, de diplomates, d'hommes d'affaires et de scientifiques, rayonne d'une diversité culturelle et d'un esprit cosmopolite par excellence. Ils ont étudié les quatre premiers semestres ensemble au département des sciences politiques de la faculté des sciences sociales et économiques, qui était, à l'époque, une des premières institutions à proposer ce genre de formation en Europe et où, surtout dans les années soixante-dix et quatre-vingt, avaient enseigné les spécialistes des sciences politiques américains et européens les plus réputés. Aujourd'hui encore, cet institut créé par le célèbre professeur Dusan Sidjanski jouit d'une excellente réputation due, notamment, au fait qu'il

Gemeinsame Studien in Genf

rbgroßherzog Henri und Maria Teresa lernen sich zu Beginn ihres Studiums im Jahre 1975 in Genf kennen, einer Stadt, die mit ihrer interessanten Mischung von internationalen Beamten, Diplomaten, Geschäftsleuten und Wissenschaftlern kulturelle Vielfalt und kosmopolitische Gesinnung par excellence ausstrahlt und vermittelt. Sie studierten die ersten vier Semester gemeinsam am Departement für politische Wissenschaften der sozial- und wirtschaftswissenschaftlichen Fakultät, das damals zu den ersten institutionalisierten Studiengängen dieser Art in Europa gehörte und an dem besonders in den 70er und 80er Jahren die namhaftesten amerikanischen und europäischen Politikwissenschaftler lehrten. Bis heute genießt die von dem renommierten Professor Dusan Sidjanski gegründete Abteilung auch wegen der internationalen

Studying together in Geneva

Prince Henri and Maria Teresa first met in 1975 at the beginning of their university studies in Geneva, a city which, with its interesting mixture of international civil servants, diplomats, business people and scientists, exudes and instils a sense of cultural diversity and cosmopolitanism par excellence. They studied for the first two years in the Department of Political Science in the Faculty of Social and Economic Sciences, following one of the first institutionalized courses of that type in Europe which, especially in the seventies and eighties, was taught by some of the most eminent American and European political scientists. Down to the present day the Department, founded by the distinguished scholar Professor Dusan Sidjanski, has continued to enjoy an extremely good reputation, due in part to the international origins of its students.

attire des étudiants du monde entier.

◆ Maria Teresa, qui s'intéressait beaucoup aux questions pédagogiques, morales et sociales, y obtient son diplôme en sciences politiques après deux semestres supplémentaires portant essentiellement sur l'intégration européenne, les relations avec le Tiers monde et la philosophie politique. Elle consacra sa thèse à une comparaison de la législation applicable au travail féminin et à la maternité dans les Etats membres de la Communauté européenne dans laquelle elle analysait la compatibilité entre l'activité professionnelle de la femme et l'éducation des enfants. Elle profitait de ses loisirs pour enseigner dans une école de Genève et pour soigner les vieillards d'une maison de retraite.

◆ Le grand-duc héritier est diplômé de l'Institut des hautes études internationales de l'université de Genève, un établissement pluridisciplinaire fondé par William Rappard à l'époque de la Société des nations afin de promouvoir la solidarité internationale. Cet établissement prépare ses étudiants à une future carrière diplomatique ou à des fonctions supérieures dans le domaine politique ou industriel en leur enseignant une philosophie aussi étendue que possible de la coopération européenne et mondiale. Au cours de ses études, le prince Henri s'intéressa non seulement à l'intégra-

Herkunft seiner Studenten einen sehr guten Ruf. ◆ Die sehr stark an pädagogischen, moralischen und sozialen Fragestellungen interessierte Maria Teresa schloß ihr Studium am politischen Departement nach zwei weiteren Semestern mit dem Schwerpunkt europäische Integration, Beziehungen zur Dritten Welt und politische Philosophie erfolgreich ab. Sie legte eine Abschlußarbeit über einen Vergleich der Gesetzgebung zur Frauenarbeit und zum Mutterschutz in der Europäischen Gemeinschaft vor, in der sie sich mit der Vereinbarkeit von Mutterschaft und Berufsarbeit auseinandersetzte. In ihrer Freizeit unterrichtete sie an einer Genfer Schule und sie kümmerte sich um ältere Menschen in einem Altersheim. ◆ Der Erbgroßherzog ist Absolvent des „Instituts für hohe internationale Studien" der Universität Genf, ein pluridisziplinäres Institut, das zur Zeit des Völkerbundes von William Rappard zur Förderung der internationalen Solidarität gegründet wurde. Durch eine möglichst umfassende Betrachtung der europäischen und internationalen Zusammenarbeit sollen die Studenten hier für eine spätere Diplomatenlaufbahn oder für eine Karriere in einer hohen politischen oder wirtschaftlichen Funktion vorbereitet werden. Während seines Grundstudiums beschäftigte sich Prinz Henri neben

◆ Keenly interested in educational, moral and social issues, Maria Teresa successfully completed her studies after another year in the Political Studies Department. Her special subjects were European integration, relations with the Third World and political philosophy. Her final dissertation was a comparative study on women at work and the protection of expectant and nursing mothers in the legislation of the European Community, in which she dealt with the compatibility of motherhood and gainful employment. In her free time she taught at a school in Geneva and looked after elderly people in an eventide home. ◆ The Heir Apparent is a graduate of the Institute for Higher International Studies at the University of Geneva, a multidisciplinary institute founded by William Rappard at the time of the League of Nations to promote international solidarity. The aim of the institute is to provide students with the widest possible insight into European and international cooperation, thereby preparing them for a career in the diplomatic service or for a leading role in politics or business. During his first two years of study, Prince Henri dealt with European integration, constitutional questions relating to the Benelux countries and economic policy. In the latter part of his course he mainly studied factors affecting the nature of international

tion européenne, mais aussi aux questions de droit constitutionnel dans les pays membres du Benelux et à la politique économique et, plus tard, principalement à la problématique des relations internationales. En 1980, il soutient avec succès une thèse consacrée aux conditions d'adhésion de la Grèce à la CEE. ◆ Toujours durant ses études, il effectuera des stages à l'Industrial Bank of Japan, au Japon, et à la Trade-Arbed, à New York, qui lui permirent d'acquérir une expérience utile de la pratique économique. ◆ Dès 1968, dans le cadre de sa charge officielle de grand-duc héritier, le prince Henri participera activement aux efforts du gouvernement en vue de renforcer la position du Luxembourg en tant que pôle économique. La même année, il accompagnera une mission économique aux Etats-Unis et, l'année suivante, il séjournera assez longuement en Corée du Sud à l'occasion de l'ouverture de la société Trefil-Arbed Korea. ◆ Peu de temps après avoir brillamment achevé leurs études, le grand-duc héritier Henri et Maria Teresa se marièrent le 14 février 1981; ils vivent depuis lors au Luxembourg avec leurs enfants.

der europäischen Integration mit verfassungsrechtlichen Fragen in den Beneluxländern sowie mit Wirtschaftspolitik und später hauptsächlich mit Fragen, die den Charakter der internationalen Beziehungen berühren. Im Jahre 1980 legte er seine Abschlußarbeit über die Beitrittsbedingungen Griechenlands für die Aufnahme in die Europäische Wirtschaftsgemeinschaft vor. ◆ Noch zur Zeit seines Genfer Aufenthaltes schloß er Praktika bei der „Industrial Bank of Japan" in Japan und bei der „Trade Arbed" in New York ab, die ihm einen wertvollen Einblick in die wirtschaftliche Praxis vermittelten. ◆ In seiner offiziellen Funktion als Erbgroßherzog nahm Prinz Henri bereits seit 1978 aktiv an den Bemühungen der Regierung zur Stärkung des wirtschaftlichen Standortes Luxemburg teil. Noch im gleichen Jahr begleitete er eine Wirtschaftsdelegation nach Amerika und ein Jahr später führte ihn ein längerer Aufenthalt im Rahmen der Eröffnung von Trefil-Arbed Korea nach Südkorea. ◆ Kurz nach ihren erfolgreichen Studienabgängen heirateten Erbgroßherzog Henri und Maria Teresa am 14. Februar 1981; seitdem leben sie mit ihren Kindern in Luxemburg.

relations. In 1980 he submitted a dissertation on the conditions for the accession of Greece to the European Community. ◆ While at Geneva University he underwent practical training in Japan with the Industrial Bank of Japan and in New York with Trade Arbed, which gave him valuable experience of business practice. ◆ In his official role as heir apparent, Prince Henri had been actively assisting the efforts of the Government to enhance the appeal of Luxembourg as a business location since 1978. In that year he accompanied a business delegation to the United States and a year later he had a lengthy stay in South Korea in connection with the opening of Trefil-Arbed Korea. ◆ Soon after obtaining their degrees, Prince Henri and Maria Teresa were married on 14 February 1981, since when they have lived in Luxembourg and have brought five children into the world.

- Mariage le 14 février 1981, jour de la Saint-Valentin. La veille, le prince était allé accueillir sa fiancée à la frontière franco-luxembourgeoise.

- Vermählung am Valentinstag, dem 14. Februar 1981. Am Vorabend hatte der Prinz seine Verlobte an der französisch-luxemburgischen Grenze empfangen.

- Marriage on St Valentine's Day, 14 February 1981. On the eve of the wedding, the Prince had gone to greet his fiancée at the Franco-Luxembourg border

Les tâches officielles

Die offiziellen Aufgaben

Official duties

a dynastie exerce diverses fonctions représentatives dans la monarchie constitutionnelle et parlementaire du Luxembourg sans intervenir directement dans le processus décisionnel qui rassemble le gouvernement, le Parlement, le Conseil d'État et les groupements d'intérêts. Comme en témoigne le succès de foule des apparitions solennelles de la famille du grand-duc ou du grand-duc héritier, notamment à l'occasion des cérémonies de la Fête nationale, cet effacement politique ne doit pourtant pas faire croire que l'institution monarchique ne contribue pas grandement à l'identité et à la continuité de la société luxembourgeoise. ◆ L'importance du rôle que la monarchie joue en combinaison avec les autres institutions s'explique surtout par son impartialité. Personnification la plus visible de l'idée nationale, le couple grand-ducal appa-

ie Dynastie nimmt in der konstitutionellen und parlamentarischen Monarchie Luxemburgs verschiedene repräsentative Funktionen wahr, ohne aktiv in den politischen Entscheidungsprozeß zwischen Regierung, Parlament, Staatsrat und Interessenorganisationen einzugreifen. Wie die feierlichen und von der Bevölkerung zahlreich besuchten Auftritte der großherzoglichen und erbgroßherzoglichen Familie zum Beispiel bei den Feierlichkeiten zum Nationalfeiertag zeigen, darf diese politische Zurückhaltung jedoch nicht über den wichtigen Beitrag dieser Institution zur Identität und Kontinuität der luxemburgischen Gesellschaft hinwegtäuschen. ◆ Ihre wichtige Rolle im Zusammenspiel mit den anderen Institutionen erklärt sich hauptsächlich aus ihrem überparteilichen Charakter: Als sichtbarste Verkörperung der natio-

he dynasty has a representative role to play in the constitutional monarchy and parliamentary democracy of Luxembourg but does not become actively involved in the decision-making process in which the Government, Parliament, the Council of State and organizations representing particular interests take part. As is shown by the formal appearances of the grand ducal family and the heir's family on state occasions, such as the festivities marking the National Day on 23 June, which are attended by large numbers of the population, this political restraint must not delude anyone into underestimating the importance of the monarchy as a means of identification and a source of continuity for Luxembourg society. ◆ The importance of the monarchy's role in its interaction with the other national institutions stems mainly from its impartial nature.

raît comme le représentant de tous les Luxembourgeois; par contre, même le Premier ministre ou, d'une façon générale, un chef d'État élu ne jouit jamais que de la faveur d'une majorité de la population. L'exercice de cette fonction d'intégration nationale, qui s'exprime notamment lors des nombreux devoirs de représentation du grand-duc héritier Henri et de la grande-duchesse héritière Maria Teresa (audiences, participation à des fêtes de bienfaisance, inauguration d'expositions, participation à des séances académiques), revêt une importance particulière pour un petit pays comme le Luxembourg, où les allochtones représentent aujourd'hui plus d'un tiers de la population. ◆ Notamment en raison de leur aura discrète et de leur effacement privé, le prince Henri et la princesse Maria Teresa sont, au Luxembourg comme à l'étranger, des personnalités très appréciées et respectées; avec leur conception responsable et moderne de leur fonction, ils remplissent déjà de nombreux devoirs dans l'intérêt de leur pays. Leurs activités multiples et diversifiées comprennent entre autres l'exercice de plus de trente présidences d'honneur, présidences et patronages qui couvrent tous les aspects de la vie sociale; ces tâches les obligent parfois à participer activement aux travaux des organismes concernés, à échanger des idées

nalen Idee tritt das erbgroßherzogliche Paar als Repräsentant aller Luxemburger auf; demgegenüber kann sogar der Premierminister und in der Regel auch ein gewähltes Staatsoberhaupt seine Gunst immer nur auf eine Bevölkerungsmehrheit stützen. Die Wahrnehmung dieser nationalen Integrationsfunktion, die auch anläßlich der vielen Repräsentationspflichten von Erbgroßherzog Henri und Erbgroßherzogin Maria Teresa (Audienzen, Besuch von Wohltätigkeitsveranstaltungen, Eröffnung von Ausstellungen, Teilnahme an akademischen Sitzungen) zum Ausdruck kommt, ist von besonderer Bedeutung für ein kleines Land wie Luxemburg, das heute einen nicht-luxemburgischen Bevölkerungsanteil von über 33% aufweist. ◆ Nicht zuletzt wegen ihrer diskreten Ausstrahlung und ihrer privaten Zurückhaltung sind Prinz Henri und Prinzessin Maria Teresa sowohl im In- als auch im Ausland hochangesehen und respektierte Persönlichkeiten, die mit ihrem verantwortungsbewußten und modernen Amtsverständnis bereits vielfältige Aufgaben im Interesse des Landes wahrnehmen. Zu ihrem umfassenden und breitgefächerten Aufgabenbereich gehören die Ausübung von über 30 Ehrenpräsidentschaften, Präsidentschaften und Schirmherrschaften, die sich über sämtliche gesellschaftliche Belange er-

The Prince and Princess, as the most visible embodiment of the nation, represent all Luxembourgers; by contrast, even the Prime Minister and, as a rule, an elected head of state depend solely on the approval of a majority of the population. The fulfilment of this national integrating function, which is also seen in the official engagements undertaken by the Heir Apparent and Princess Maria Teresa (audiences, visits to charity events, opening of exhibitions, attendance at academic meetings), is especially important to a small country such as Luxembourg, which now counts 33% non-natives among its population. ◆ Not least because of the air of discretion they convey and their restrained private lifestyle, Prince Henri and Princess Maria Teresa are admired and respected both at home and abroad; with their responsible and modern perception of their calling, they already perform a wide variety of duties on behalf of their country. Their comprehensive and kaleidoscopic list of responsibilities includes more than 30 positions as honorary president, president or patron of organizations in every area of social concern, some of which involve a considerable commitment, and exchanges of views with leading representatives of economic, political and cultural bodies, meetings with important guests from Luxembourg and

avec des personnalités du monde économique, politique et culturel, à rencontrer des hôtes de marque luxembourgeois et étranger, à répondre à des requêtes ou à d'autres lettres provenant du pays et de l'étranger ou, en ce qui concerne le grand-duc héritier Henri, à remettre chaque année leur diplôme aux jeunes maîtres-artisans. ◆ Pour faire face à ces devoirs, le couple princier peut compter sur les dizaines d'années d'expérience et sur les conseils du grand-duc Jean et de la grande-duchesse Joséphine-Charlotte; cette relation de confiance est surtout importante pour les successeurs désignés à cette haute fonction. ◆ La multiplicité des tâches princières dans le domaine culturel, social, économique et sportif exige l'étude approfondie de toutes sortes de thèmes et une présence physique marquée dans toutes les contrées du pays. Cette proximité du peuple explique aussi en bonne partie la grande popularité du prince Henri et de la princesse Maria Teresa. ◆ Parmi les activités primordiales du prince Henri figure son importante fonction dans les missions extérieures du ministère de l'Économie et des Affaires étrangères en faveur du renforcement de l'économie luxembourgeoise. En tant que président du «Board of Economic Development» (cette charge est assumée par

strecken und die zum Teil sehr engagierte Mitarbeit in diesen Organen sowie der Meinungsaustausch mit hohen wirtschaftlichen, politischen und kulturellen Vertretern, die Begegnung mit hohen luxemburgischen und ausländischen Gästen, die Beantwortung von Bittbriefen oder sonstiger Korrespondenz aus dem In- und Ausland oder die alljährliche Diplomüberreichung an die jungen Handwerksmeister durch Erbgroßherzog Henri. Bei der Bewältigung dieser Aufgaben kann sich das erbgroßherzogliche Paar auf die jahrzehntelange Erfahrung und auf die Ratschläge von Großherzog Jean und Großherzogin Joséphine-Charlotte stützen, - eine verläßliche Beziehung, die besonders für die Nachfolger in diesem hohen Amt von Bedeutung ist. Die sehr unterschiedlichen Tätigkeiten im kulturellen, sozialen, wirtschaftlichen und sportlichen Bereich erfordern eine zeitintensive Beschäftigung und Auseinandersetzung mit allen möglichen Themen wie auch eine starke physische Präsenz in allen Gegenden des Landes. Die große Beliebtheit von Prinz Henri und Prinzessin Maria Teresa ist auch zu einem guten Teil auf diese Volksnähe zurückzuführen. Zu den herausragenden Tätigkeiten von Erbgroßherzog Henri gehört seine wichtige Funktion bei den Auslandsmissionen des Wirt-

abroad, replying to petitions or other correspondence from within and outside the country, the Heir Apparent's annual presentation of masters' diplomas to young craftsmen, and so forth. As they go about their duties, the couple can draw on the decades of experience and the advice of Grand Duke Jean and Grand Duchess Joséphine-Charlotte – a reliable source of assistance which is especially valued by the heirs to their distinguished office. ◆ Their wide range of diverse activities in the cultural, social, economic and sporting domains necessitate time-consuming consideration and analysis of all sorts of topics as well as frequent physical presence in all areas of the country. The immense popularity of Prince Henri and Princess Maria Teresa, indeed, is due in large measure to their closeness to the people. ◆ One of Prince Henri's foremost activities is the important function he performs on trade missions undertaken by the Ministry of Economic and Foreign Affairs for the purpose of strengthening the Luxembourg economy. As President of the Board of Economic Development – since the creation of the Board of Industrial Development in 1960, the presidency has been held by a member of the grand ducal family – he and the Economics Minister jointly head the regular delegations to North America and Asia.

un membre de la famille grand-ducale depuis la création du «Board of Industrial Development» en 1960), il dirige, en compagnie du ministre de l'Économie, les voyages d'étude qui ont lieu régulièrement en Amérique du Nord et en Asie. Ses excellentes relations ont permis l'implantation de nombreuses entreprises nouvelles au Luxembourg et donc la création de nouveaux emplois. L'influence du grand-duc héritier Henri, qui se fonde sur son prestige et sur son expérience, s'exerce aussi dans le cadre des missions économiques que le ministère du Commerce extérieur organise avec des délégations de banques et d'entreprises luxembourgeoises ou établies au Grand-Duché. ◆ Depuis 1980, le prince Henri est membre du Conseil d'État, un organe consultatif (mais dont la consultation est obligatoire) qui est chargé de sanctionner tous les textes de loi. Il participe régulièrement aux séances de cette institution qui ont lieu tous les quinze jours, et plus particulièrement aux travaux de la commission des questions institutionnelles. ◆ Au plan international, le prince s'occupe spécialement des questions sociales et écologiques. Avec la reine Silvia de Suède, il compte notamment parmi les membres fondateurs de la fondation privée Mentor, créée en 1994 à Genève afin de lutter pour la prévention de l'abus

schafts- und Außenministeriums zur Stärkung der luxemburgischen Wirtschaft. Als Präsident des „Board of Economic Development" - diese Aufgabe wird seit der Schaffung des „Board of Industrial Development" im Jahre 1960 von einem Mitglied der großherzoglichen Familie wahrgenommen - leitet er in Begleitung des Wirtschaftsministers die regelmäßig stattfindenden Reisen nach Nordamerika und Asien. So gelang mit der Hilfe seiner guten Kontakte die Ansiedlung von zahlreichen neuen Industrien in Luxemburg und die damit verbundene Schaffung neuer Arbeitsplätze. Auch bei den Wirtschaftsmissionen des Außenhandelsministers mit Delegationen luxemburgischer und in Luxemburg angesiedelter Banken und Unternehmen kann Erbgroßherzog Henri sein auf Amt und Erfahrung beruhendes Gewicht geltend machen. Seit 1980 ist Prinz Henri Mitglied des Staatsrates, ein konsultatives, aber obligatorisch zu konsultierendes Organ, das sein Gutachten zu sämtlichen Gesetzestexten abgeben muß. Er nimmt regelmäßig an den vierzehntägig stattfindenden Sitzungen teil und arbeitet insbesondere in der Kommission für institutionelle Fragen mit. ◆ Auf internationaler Ebene engagiert sich der Prinz besonders für soziale und ökologische Themen. Er gehört neben Königin Silvia von Schweden u.a. zu den

Prince Henri's useful contacts have helped to bring about the establishment of numerous new industries in Luxembourg, thereby bringing new jobs to the country. Similarly, when the Minister for External Trade travels with delegations from Luxembourg-based banks and businesses, Prince Henri is able to lend them the influence that derives from his position and experience. ◆ Since 1980 Prince Henri has been a member of the Council of State, a consultative body but one whose opinion must be sought before any legislation can be enacted. He regularly attends its fortnightly meetings and is a member of its Commission on Institutional Matters. ◆ Internationally, the Prince is especially committed to social and environmental causes. Along with Queen Silvia of Sweden, he is one of the founder members of the private Mentor Foundation, established in Geneva in 1994, which works worldwide to prevent the abuse of legal and illegal drugs by young people. In collaboration with the World Health Organization, Mentor organizes conferences and seminars; the Foundation also supports pilot preventive projects in three different continents. ◆ A second issue to which Prince Henri devotes special attention is the Galapagos archipelago, a unique biotope where the ecological balance is threatened as a result of human in-

de drogues légales et illégales chez les jeunes du monde entier. Mentor organise entre autres des colloques et des séminaires en collaboration avec l'Organisation mondiale de la santé; en outre, la fondation soutient des projets pilotes en matière de prévention dans trois continents différents. ◆ Le deuxième sujet qui préoccupe particulièrement le prince est l'archipel des Galapagos, un groupe d'îles du Pacifique qui abritent un biotope unique au monde et dont l'équilibre écologique est menacé par l'activité humaine. C'est sous la présidence de Henri que l'association «The Galapagos Darwin Trust», une branche de la «Charles Darwin Foundation for the Galapagos Islands» fondée en 1959, a été créée au Luxembourg en 1990 pour financer des mesures de protection de l'environnement et de sensibilisation et pour promouvoir la recherche scientifique en vue de préserver la diversité biologique dans les îles concernées. En 1972, l'Unesco avait classé l'archipel des Galapagos en tant que patrimoine de l'humanité à protéger tout spécialement. ◆ En plus de ces deux activités au sein d'organisations non gouvernementales internationales, qui l'obligent à travailler intensément pour préparer des réunions de comité directeur qui se tiennent le plus souvent à l'étranger, le grand-duc héritier patronne aussi

Gründungsmitgliedern der 1994 in Genf geschaffenen privaten Mentor-Stiftung, die sich weltweit für die Vorbeugung gegen den Mißbrauch von legalen und illegalen Drogen bei Jugendlichen einsetzt. In Zusammenarbeit mit der Weltgesundheitsorganisation organisiert Mentor Konferenzen und Seminare; des weiteren unterstützt die Stiftung präventive Pilotprojekte auf drei verschiedenen Kontinenten. ◆ Ein zweites Thema, das Prinz Henri besonders beschäftigt, ist die im Pazifik gelegene Galápagos-Inselgruppe, ein weltweit einzigartiges Biotop, dessen ökologisches Gleichgewicht als Folge von menschlichen Eingriffen bedroht ist. Unter seiner Präsidentschaft wurde im Jahre 1990 in Luxemburg der Verein „The Galápagos Darwin Trust" gegründet, eine Unterorganisation der 1959 entstandenen „Charles Darwin Foundation for the Galápagos Islands", die sich durch die Finanzierung von Naturschutz- und Sensibilisierungsmaßnahmen sowie die Förderung von wissenschaftlicher Forschung für die Erhaltung der Artenvielfalt auf diesen Inseln einsetzt. Im Jahre 1972 wurde die Inselgruppe von der Unesco als besonders schützenswertes Menschheitserbe eingestuft. ◆ Neben diesen beiden aktiven Tätigkeiten in internationalen, nicht-staatlichen Organisationen, die eine intensive Vor-

terference. Under his presidency the Galapagos Darwin Trust was founded in Luxembourg in 1990 as a subsidiary body of the Charles Darwin Foundation for the Galapagos Islands, created in 1959 to work for the preservation of the islands' biodiversity by financing protection and awareness programmes and promoting scientific research. In 1972 the archipelago was added by Unesco to the World Heritage List as a natural site of outstanding universal value. ◆ Besides these two areas of active involvement in international non-governmental organizations, requiring painstaking preparation of board meetings, most of which are held abroad, the Heir Apparent is also the patron of nume-

de nombreuses associations culturelles, humanitaires et sportives qui se sont distinguées par des mérites particuliers sur le plan national. La protection civile, le «Rotary Club» luxembourgeois, le comité luxembourgeois de l'Unicef ou l'association luxembourgeoise pour la promotion des sports d'hiver n'en sont que quelques exemples. ◆ Le prince Henri est directeur honoris causa de la «Sacred Heart University Fairfield» (États-Unis) depuis 1992 et de la «Miami University Oxford» depuis 1993. Le même titre lui a été décerné par l'université de Kon Kaen, en Thaïlande, et par l'université de Trèves en 1996. ◆ L'essentiel des activités de la grande-duchesse héritière Maria Teresa touchent au domaine social et humanitaire. En étroite collaboration avec les ministères de la Santé, de l'Éducation, de la Jeunesse et de la Famille, elle visite régulièrement des institutions établies et nouvelles. Aidée par une conscience sociale développée, une connaissance précise des dossiers et un sens aigu du dialogue, elle cherche à acquérir ainsi une image aussi complète et fidèle que possible de la société luxembourgeoise sans en occulter les points faibles. ◆ Elle s'efforce de mettre en pratique ces connaissances concrètes en s'impliquant directement dans la Fondation Prince Henri - Princesse Maria Te-

bereitung der meistens im Ausland stattfindenden Vorstandssitzungen erfordern, hat der Erbgroßherzog noch zahlreiche Schirmherrschaften von kulturellen, humanitären und sportlichen Organisationen inne, die sich durch besondere Verdienste auf nationaler Ebene bewährt haben. Als Beispiele sind nur der nationale Zivilschutz, der Luxemburger „Rotary", das Luxemburger Unicef-Komitee oder der Luxemburger Wintersportverband genannt.

Prinz Henri ist seit 1992 Ehrendoktor der „Sacred Heart University Fairfield" (USA); 1993 erhielt er die Ehrendoktorwürde der „Miami University Oxford". Im Jahre 1996 folgte die Verleihung des Ehrendoktors der Kon Kaen Universität in Thailand und der Universität Trier.

Der Schwerpunkt der Tätigkeiten von Erbgroßherzogin Maria Teresa konzentriert sich auf den sozialen und humanitären Bereich. In enger Zusammenarbeit mit dem Gesundheits-, Unterrichts-, Jugend- oder Familienministerium besucht sie regelmäßig bestehende und neu entstandene Einrichtungen. Mit Hilfe ihres ausgeprägten sozialen Bewußtseins, eines genauen Aktenstudiums und eines gezielten Meinungsaustausches ist sie auf diese Weise bestrebt, sich ein möglichst vollständiges und reales Bild von der luxemburgischen Gesellschaft zu machen, das auch deren

rous cultural, humanitarian and sporting organizations. The National Civil Defence Organization, the Luxembourg Rotary Club, the Luxembourg Unicef Committee and the Luxembourg Winter Sports Federation are but a few examples. ◆ Since 1992 Prince Henri has been an honorary doctor of the Sacred Heart University of Fairfield in the United States, in 1993 an honorary doctorate was conferred on him by Miami University in Oxford, Ohio, and in 1996 he received honorary doctorates from the Kon Kaen University in Thailand and the University of Trier in Germany. ◆ The main focal points of Princess Maria Teresa's activities are the social and humanitarian domains. In close cooperation with the Ministries of Health, Education, Youth and Families, she regularly visits existing and newly created establishments. With the aid of her undoubted social awareness, her careful study of background material and her talks with experts in these domains, she seeks to form in her own mind as complete and accurate a picture as possible of Luxembourg society, warts and all. ◆ Armed with this specific knowledge, she tries to put it to good use through her direct involvement in the work of the Prince Henri-Princess Maria Teresa Foundation and in the Luxembourg Forum on Childhood and Youth, which was establi-

resa et dans le Forum de l'enfance et de la jeunesse luxembourgeoises qui a vu le jour en 1995. La fondation qui porte le nom du couple princier a été créée en 1981; placée sous la présidence de la princesse, dont les idées foisonnantes lui fournissent une impulsion essentielle, elle œuvre en faveur de l'intégration des personnes handicapées et défavorisées. Grâce à ses moyens financiers, à ses campagnes de sensibilisation et au prix qu'elle décerne en reconnaissance de mérites exceptionnels tels que la création d'une infrastructure adaptée aux handicapés, cette organisation a contribué à sensibiliser davantage les gens aux conséquences des différents types de handicaps. ◆ D'autre part, la princesse Maria Teresa est particulièrement attentive à l'enfance déshéritée dans notre société. Dans le cadre du forum pluridisciplinaire pour l'enfance et la jeunesse que patronne sa fondation, elle étudie, avec des psychiatres, des pédagogues, des juristes, des psychologues et des assistants sociaux, tous les problèmes et les souffrances des enfants victimes notamment de la maltraitance sexuelle ou de la prostitution. Dans ce contexte, c'est elle qui a dirigé la délégation luxembourgeoise au congrès mondial sur l'exploitation sexuelle des enfants à des fins commerciales, qui s'est tenu en 1996 à Stockholm; elle a activement parti-

Schwachstellen nicht verkennt. Dieses konkrete Wissen versucht sie durch ihren direkten Einsatz in der „Prince Henri-Princesse Maria Teresa Stiftung" und dem seit 1995 bestehenden „Luxemburger Kinder- und Jugendforum" umzusetzen. Die 1981 gegründete Stiftung, die den Namen des erbgroßherzoglichen Paares trägt, setzt sich unter der Präsidentschaft von Prinzessin Maria Teresa, die der Organisation mit ihren vielen Ideen einen wichtigen Impuls gibt, für eine verbesserte Integration von behinderten und benachteiligten Mitbürgern ein. Mit ihren finanziellen Mitteln, ihren Sensibilisierungskampagnen und der Verleihung eines Preises für besondere Verdienste, so beispielsweise für die Schaffung einer behindertengerechten Infrastruktur, hat diese Stiftung dazu beigetragen, das Bewußtsein für die Folgen von jedwelcher Benachteiligung zu schärfen. ◆ Eine besondere Sensibilität bringt Prinzessin Maria Teresa außerdem den notdürftigen Kindern in unserer Gesellschaft entgegen. In dem unter der Schirmherrschaft der Stiftung stehenden multidisziplinären Forum für die Kindheit und Jugend setzt sie sich mit Psychiatern, Pädagogen, Juristen, Psychologen, Sozialhelfern mit allen Problemen und Leiden von Kindern wie sexueller Mißbrauch oder Prostitution auseinander. In diesem Zusammenhang

shed in 1995. The foundation bearing the names of the Prince and Princess strives for better integration of the disabled and disadvantaged and benefits from the stimulus lent it by its president, Princess Maria Teresa, with her wealth of innovative ideas. By providing financial resources, conducting public awareness campaigns and awarding a prize for special achievements, for example the creation of infrastructural facilities based on the needs of disabled people, the foundation has helped to focus public awareness on the consequences of any type of handicap. ◆ In addition, Princess Maria Teresa is acutely aware of the plight of needy children in our society. In the multidisciplinary Forum on Childhood and Youth, she meets with psychiatrists, educationalists, lawyers, psychologists and social workers to discuss all the problems and suffering faced by children, such as sexual abuse and prostitution. In 1996 she headed the Luxembourg delegation to the international congress in Stockholm on the sexual exploitation of children for commercial purposes. Together with the Families Minister, she plays an active role in the various working groups. ◆ Besides these two very demanding and strenuous activities, Princess Maria Teresa is also the patron of other organizations, such as the Aids Research Foundation, the

cipé aux réflexions des groupes de travail en compagnie du ministre de la Famille. ◆ A côté de ces deux activités exigeantes et complexes, la princesse Maria Teresa patronne encore notamment la Fondation pour la recherche sur le sida, l'Association des aveugles luxembourgeois, la société Alzheimer du Luxembourg et, dans le domaine culturel, le Festival européen du théâtre et de la musique de Wiltz.

leitete sie im Jahre 1996 die luxemburgische Delegation, die am Weltkongreß über sexuelle Ausbeutung von Kindern zu kommerziellen Zwecken in Stockholm teilnahm. Zusammen mit der Familienministerin arbeitete sie aktiv in den Arbeitsgruppen mit. ◆ Neben diesen beiden sehr anspruchsvollen und arbeitsintensiven Aktivitäten hat Prinzessin Maria Teresa noch unter anderen die Schirmherrschaft über die Stiftung zur Aidsforschung, die Luxemburger Blindenvereinigung, die Luxemburger Alzheimer Gesellschaft und im kulturellen Bereich über das Europäische Theater- und Musikfestival in Wiltz.

Luxembourg Association of the Blind, the Luxembourg Alzheimer Society and, in the cultural sphere, the European Festival of Music and Drama in Wiltz.

▦ *Pages suivantes:*
La Fête nationale luxembourgeoise, dont la date a été fixée au 23 juin, célèbre l'anniversaire officiel du Grand-Duc.

▦ *Auf den folgenden Seiten:*
Mit dem Luxemburger Nationalfeiertag am 23. Juni wird der Geburtstag des Großherzogs offiziell gefeiert

■ *Following pages:*
The twenty-third of June has been established as the National Day in Luxembourg, when the Grand Duke's official birthday is celebrated

■ *Sur les deux pages précédentes:*
À Echternach, le couple princier assiste à la procession dansante qui, chaque mardi de Pentecôte depuis des temps immémoriaux, passe devant le tombeau de saint Willibrord au son des fanfares

■ *Auf den beiden vorherigen Seiten:*
Das Prinzenpaar wohnt der Echternacher Springprozession bei, die seit Jahrhunderten jeden Pfingstdienstag zu den Klängen der Musikkapellen am Grab des hl. Willibrord vorbeizieht

■ *Previous two pages:*
The Prince and Princess attending the dancing procession which, every year on the Tuesday after Pentecost (Whit Tuesday) since time immemorial, goes past the tomb of Saint Willibrord in Echternach, accompanied by the music of brass bands

■ En août 1986, à l'âge de quatre ans, le prince Guillaume baptise le Metroliner III de Luxair qui portera son nom

■ Im August 1986 tauft der vierjährige Prinz Guillaume den Luxair-Metroliner III, der seinen Namen trägt

■ In August 1986, at the age of four, Prince Guillaume christens the Luxair Metroliner III which is to bear his name

Centre d'instruction militaire du Härebierg en mars 1984. Depuis l'abandon de la conscription en 1967, l'armée luxembourgeoise est uniquement composée de volontaires. Forte d'environ 700 hommes, dont une compagnie de reconnaissance de l'OTAN, elle est basée sur la colline du Härebierg près de Diekirch.

Das Militärausbildungszentrum des „Härebierg" im März 1984. Seit die Wehrpflicht 1967 aufgehoben wurde, besteht die Luxemburger Armee nur noch aus Freiwilligen. Die Armee ist – einschließlich eines NATO-Aufklärungstrupps – rund 700 Mann stark und hat ihre Basis auf dem „Härebierg" bei Diekirch.

Härebierg military training centre in March 1984. Since conscription was abolished in 1967, the Luxembourg army has consisted entirely of volunteers. With a strength of around 700 men, including a NATO reconnaissance company, it is based on the hill at Härebierg, near Diekirch.

■ *Pages précédentes:* Carmel, Californie, en septembre 1987

Vorherige Seiten: Carmel, Kalifornien, im September 1987

■ *Previous pages:* Carmel, California, in September 1987

■ Italie, juillet 1988. Le couple princier assiste au *Palio*, la traditionnelle course de chevaux, qui se déroule chaque été sur la Piazza del Campo à Sienne.
À Florence, les princes ne manquent pas d'aller saluer le *Porcellino*, porte-bonheur sur le Mercato Nuovo. Ils assistent à Milan à une soirée donnée par M. Giovanni Agnelli. À Maranello, le prince Henri ressent des émotions fortes en effectuant quelques tours de piste sur le circuit Ferrari.

Italien, Juli 1988. Das Prinzenpaar besucht den *Palio*, das traditionsreiche Pferderennen, das jeden Sommer auf der Piazza del Campo in Siena stattfindet.
In Florenz machen Prinz Henri und Prinzessin Maria Teresa dem *Porcellino* ihre Aufwartung, dem Glücksbringer auf dem Mercato Nuovo. In Mailand wohnen sie einem Empfang von Giovanni Agnelli bei. In Maranello dreht Prinz Henri begeistert einige Runden auf der Ferrari-Rennstrecke.

■ Italy, July 1988. The Prince and Princess attend the *Palio*, the traditional horse race held every year on the Piazza del Campo in Siena.
In Florence, the Prince and Princess remember to pay their respects to the *Porcellino*, the source of good luck on the Mercato Nuovo. In Milan they attend a reception given by Signor Giovanni Agnelli. At Maranello, Prince Henri feels the adrenalin flowing as he does a few rounds of the Ferrari circuit.

■ Le prince Henri assiste le 11 décembre 1988 au lancement du premier satellite ASTRA à Kourou et, accompagné des principaux responsables d'Arianespace, annonce dans la salle Jupiter la réussite du vol V27. Il met à profit son séjour en Guyane pour visiter l'île du Diable, l'un des îlots de l'archipel des îles du Salut où s'est élevé un bagne de 1852 à 1936.

■ Am 11. Dezember 1988 wohnt Prinz Henri in Kourou dem Start des ersten ASTRA-Satelliten bei und gibt in Begleitung der Hauptverantwortlichen von Arianespace im Jupiter-Saal das Gelingen des Flugs V27 bekannt. Er nutzt seinen Aufenthalt in Französisch-Guyana, um die berühmte Teufelsinsel zu besuchen, eine der Inseln des Archipels der „Iles du Salut", auf der von 1852 bis 1936 Strafgefangene festgehalten wurden.

■ On 11 December 1988, the Prince attends the launch of the first ASTRA satellite at Kourou and in the Jupiter Room, accompanied by the heads of Arianespace, announces the successful completion of flight V27. He used his trip to French Guiana to visit Devils Island, one of the Iles du Salut, a penal colony from 1852 to 1936.

■ *À droite en bas:* Visite au château de Betzdorf, siège de la Société européenne des satellites (SES), où le centre de contrôle des satellites ASTRA est installé depuis 1987

■ *Rechts unten:* Besuch auf Schloß Betzdorf, Sitz der Société européenne des satellites (SES), wo sich seit 1987 das Kontrollzentrum der ASTRA-Satelliten befindet

■ *Bottom right:* Visit to the Château de Betzdorf, seat of the Société européenne des satellites (SES), where the control centre for the ASTRA satellites has been housed since 1987

Pages suivantes:
Le centenaire de la dynastie a été célébré en 1990. Sur les photos prises à la Chambre des députés lors des cérémonies officielles on reconnaît notamment Mme Erna Hennicot-Schoepges, alors présidente de la Chambre des députés et M. Jacques Santer, alors premier ministre et président du gouvernement.

Auf den folgenden Seiten:
1990 feierte die Dynastie ihr hundertjähriges Bestehen. Auf den Fotos in der Abgeordnetenkammer während der offiziellen Zeremonie: die damalige Kammerpräsidentin Erna Hennicot-Schoepges und Jacques Santer, damals Luxemburgs Premierminister und Regierungschef

Following pages:
The centenary of the dynasty was celebrated in 1990. Among those who feature in the photographs taken at the Chamber of Deputies during the official ceremonies are Erna Hennicot-Schoepges, who was President of the Chamber at that time, and Jacques Santer, who, as Prime Minister, was head of the Luxembourg Government.

Fischbach, mai 1997.
Toute la famille reçoit de jeunes enfants atteints du cancer.

Fischbach, Mai 1997.
Die Familie empfängt krebskranke Kinder.

Fischbach, May 1997.
The whole family play host to young children suffering from cancer.

84

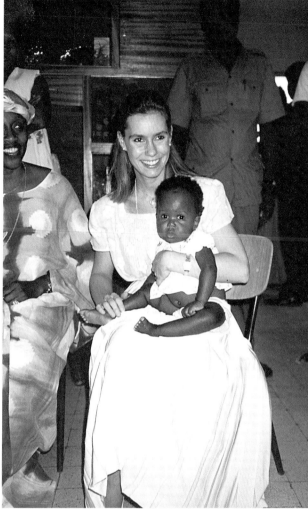

■ Sénégal, octobre 1987.
Inauguration d'un hôpital à Saint-Louis.

■ Senegal, Oktober 1987. Einweihung eines
Krankenhauses in Saint-Louis.

■ Senegal, October 1987. Official opening
of a hospital in Saint-Louis.

■ Sur la place d'Armes à Luxembourg,
la princesse Maria Teresa en compagnie des
participants luxembourgeois aux Paralympics,
John Schreiner et Henri Kaudé

■ Prinzessin Maria Teresa in Begleitung der
Luxemburger Teilnehmer der „Paralympics",
John Schreiner und Henri Kaudé, auf der Place
d'Armes

■ On the Place d'Armes in Luxembourg, Princess
Maria Teresa in the company of Luxembourg
Paralympics competitors John Schreiner
and Henri Kaudé

■ Accompagné de son fils aîné, le prince Guillaume, le prince Henri visite le dernier haut fourneau traditionnel à ARBED-Belval en 1997, avant qu'il ne soit à son tour remplacé par un four électrique.

La sidérurgie luxembourgeoise est à l'origine de l'essor économique du pays et en reste un des éléments essentiels. Le groupe ARBED compte parmi les principaux groupes sidérurgiques mondiaux.

■ In Begleitung seines ältesten Sohnes Guillaume besucht Prinz Henri 1997 bei ARBED-Belval den letzten traditionellen Hochofen, bevor dieser durch ein Elektrostahlwerk ersetzt wird.

Die luxemburgische Stahlindustrie hat den Reichtum des Landes begründet und bleibt einer seiner Pfeiler. Die ARBED-Gruppe zählt zu den wichtigsten Stahlunternehmen der Welt.

■ Accompanied by Prince Guillaume, his eldest son, Prince Henri visits the last traditional blast furnace at ARBED-Belval in 1997, before it too was replaced by an electric furnace.

The iron and steel industry in Luxembourg was the source of the country's rapid economic development and retains a key role in the economy. The ARBED group is one of the world's leading iron and steel manufacturing groups.

■ Mariage à Altshausen, avec le duc de Wurtemberg
et la duchesse, née Diane de France

▨ Hochzeit in Altshausen. Der Herzog von
Württemberg und seine Ehefrau,
geborene Diane de France

■ At a wedding in Altshausen with the Duke of
Württemberg and his wife, née Diane de France

■ Trooping the Colour, 1996.
Le prince Félix avec la reine-mère d'Angleterre.

▨ Trooping the Colour, 1996.
Prinz Felix mit der Königinmutter von England.

■ Trooping the Colour, 1996.
Prince Félix with the British Queen Mother.

■ Château de Laeken, 1981

▦ Schloß Laeken, 1981

■ Château de Laeken, 1981

■ À l'occasion du mariage du prince héritier Alois de Liechtenstein et de la princesse Sophie en Bavière, en juillet 1993, avec de g. à dr.: le prince Felipe d'Espagne, la princesse Margriet et le prince Constantijn des Pays-Bas ainsi que le prince Philippe de Belgique

▦ *Anläßlich der Vermählung von Erbprinz Alois von Liechtenstein mit Prinzessin Sophie von Bayern im Juli 1993: (v.l.n.r.) Prinz Felipe von Spanien, Prinzessin Margriet und Prinz Constantijn von den Niederlanden sowie Prinz Philippe von Belgien*

■ Photograph taken at the wedding of Prince Alois, Heir Apparent of Liechtenstein, and Princess Sophie in Bavaria in July 1993 with, from left to right, Prince Felipe of Spain, Princess Margaret and Prince Constantijn of the Netherlands, as well as Prince Philippe of Belgium

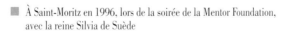

■ À Saint-Moritz en 1996, lors de la soirée de la Mentor Foundation, avec la reine Silvia de Suède

▦ *1996 in St. Moritz mit Königin Silvia von Schweden bei einem Empfang der Mentor Foundation*

■ In St. Moritz in 1996 with Queen Silvia of Sweden at a reception given by the Mentor Foundation

■ En novembre 1991, le prince de Galles remet au prince Henri sa commission de major honoraire du régiment parachutiste d'Aldershot

▦ *Im November 1991 verleiht der Prinz von Wales Prinz Henri die Ehrenmajorwürde des Fallschirmspringerregiments von Aldershot*

■ In November 1991, the Prince of Wales presents Prince Henri with his commission as an honorary major of the Parachute Regiment in Aldershot

À droite: En mars 1994, visite de l'usine Shimano au Japon.
Au milieu à droite: Pendant une mission économique au Japon en novembre 1991, le prince visite l'ancienne ville de Nara.

Rechts: Besuch der Shimano-Fabrik in Japan, März 1994.
Mitte rechts: Im Rahmen einer Wirtschaftsmission nach Japan im November 1991 besucht der Prinz die historische Stadt Nara.

Right: Visit to the Shimano factory in Japan in March 1994.
Middle right: The Prince visits the ancient town of Nara during a trade mission to Japan in November 1991.

Le grand-duc héritier et M. Yutaka Ohtoshi, président de TDK, fracassent un tonneau de sake pour libérer les esprits divins bénéfiques à l'entreprise selon une vieille tradition japonaise lors de l'ouverture de l'usine à Bascharage en octobre 1991.

En présence du gouverneur de l'État de l'Arkansas, Bill Clinton, le prince inaugure en mai 1991 l'usine TrefilARBED à Pine Bluff aux États-Unis.

Anläßlich der Fabrikeröffnung in Bascharage im Oktober 1991 zerschlagen der Erbgroßherzog und TDK-Präsident Yutaka Ohtoshi nach alter japanischer Tradition ein Sake-Faß, um die dem Unternehmen wohlgesonnenen göttlichen Geister zu befreien.

Im Beisein des damaligen Gouverneurs von Arkansas, Bill Clinton, eröffnet der Prinz im Mai 1991 die TrefilARBED-Fabrik in Pine Bluff (USA).

The Heir Apparent and Yutaka Ohtoshi, President of the TDK corporation, break a barrel of Sake to release divine spirits favourable to enterprise, in accordance with an old Japanese tradition, at the opening of the TDK factory in Bascharage in October 1991.

In the presence of Bill Clinton, who was then Governor of the State of Arkansas, the Prince opens the TrefilARBED factory in Pine Bluff, Ark.

Au mois de juin 1989, le prince se rend aux usines Fokker à Amsterdam pour inspecter un nouvel appareil commandé par Luxair.

À gauche: Lors d'une mission économique au mois de mars 1993, le prince effectue une visite de courtoisie au roi Bhumibol de Thaïlande.

Im Juni 1989 besucht der Prinz die Fokker-Produktionsstätten in Amsterdam, um eine neue, von Luxair bestellte Maschine zu begutachten.

Links: Anläßlich einer Wirtschaftsmission in Asien im März 1993 stattet der Prinz König Bhumipol von Thailand einen Höflichkeitsbesuch ab.

In June 1989, the Prince visits the Fokker works in Amsterdam to inspect a new aircraft ordered by Luxair.

Left: During a trade mission in March 1993, the Prince pays a courtesy call to King Bhumibol of Thailand.

À droite: Le 1ᵉʳ avril 1992 le grand-duc héritier est fait docteur honoris causa de la Sacred Heart University à Fairfield, Connecticut

Au milieu: Avril 1997. Visite du siège mondial de Goodyear à Akron aux États-Unis.

En bas: Mai 1995. Palo Alto, Californie. Déjeuner avec M. David Packard, co-fondateur de Hewlett-Packard.

Page de droite: Au cours d'une mission économique dans le secteur de l'audiovisuel, le prince visite en octobre 1994 les Universal Studios à Los Angeles

Rechts: Am 1. April 1992 erhält der Erbgroßherzog die Ehrendoktorwürde der Sacred Heart University in Fairfield, Connecticut (USA)

Mitte: April 1997. Besuch des Goodyear-Hauptsitzes in Akron (USA)

Unten: Mai 1995. Mit David Packard, Mitgründer von Hewlett-Packard, in Palo Alto, Kalifornien.

Rechte Seite: Der Prinz besucht im Rahmen einer Wirtschaftsmission für den audiovisuellen Sektor im Oktober 1994 die Universal Studios in Los Angeles

Right: On 1 April 1992 the Heir Apparent is awarded an honorary doctorate from the Sacred Heart University of Fairfield, Connecticut

Middle: Visit in April 1997 to the world headquarters of the Goodyear corporation at Akron in the United States

Bottom: Palo Alto, California, May 1995. Lunch with David Packard, cofounder of Hewlett-Packard.

Right page: During a trade mission undertaken by representatives of the audiovisual industries in October 1994, the Prince visits Universal Studios in Los Angeles.

93

La vie de famille

e grand-duc héritier Henri et la grande-duchesse héritière Maria Teresa accordent une importance particulière à la vie de famille. Cet attachement aux valeurs familiales ainsi que la compréhension du grand-duc Jean et de la grande-duchesse Joséphine-Charlotte pour le choix conjugal de leur fils a permis au jeune couple princier de mener une vie privée discrète. Dans ce contexte, Henri et Maria Teresa s'efforcent, grâce à des repas pris en commun ou en pratiquant des activités sportives communes, de passer le plus de temps possible avec leurs cinq enfants, le prince Guillaume (*1981), le prince Félix (*1984), le prince Louis (*1986), la princesse Alexandra (*1991) et le prince Sébastien (*1992), qui, comme les enfants de leur âge, sont scolarisés dans l'enseignement public luxembourgeois. ◆ Depuis 1987, le grand-duc héri-

Das Familienleben

ür Erbgroßherzog Henri und Erbgroßherzogin Maria Teresa nimmt das Familienleben einen besonderen Stellenwert ein. Mit Hilfe dieser familienbezogenen Einstellung wie auch mit dem Verständnis von Großherzog Jean und Großherzogin Joséphine-Charlotte für die Heiratswahl ihres Sohnes, ist es dem jungen Paar gelungen, ein diskretes Privatleben zu führen. Dabei versuchen sie vor allem durch gemeinsame Mahlzeiten und das Betreiben von gemeinsamen sportlichen Aktivitäten so viel Zeit wie möglich mit ihren fünf Kindern, Prinz Guillaume (*1981), Prinz Félix (*1984), Prinz Louis (*1986), Prinzessin Alexandra (*1991) und Prinz Sébastien (*1992) zu verbringen, die wie ihre Altersgenossen im öffentlich-luxemburgischen Schulsystem integriert sind. ◆ Seit 1987 lebt die Familie auf Schloß Fischbach in der Nähe

Family life

rince Henri and Princess Maria Teresa attach special importance to family life. Thanks to this high regard for family life and the approval given by Grand Duke Jean and Grand Duchess Joséphine-Charlotte to their son's choice of spouse, the young couple have managed to lead a discreet private life. They try to spend as much time as possible, primarily through family meals and common sporting activities, with their five children, Prince Guillaume (born 1981), Prince Félix (1984), Prince Louis (1986), Princess Alexandra (1991) and Prince Sébastien (1992), who, like their contemporaries, attend state schools in Luxembourg. ◆ Since 1987 the family has lived in the Château de Fischbach, near Mersch, from where the Heir Apparent and Princess Maria Teresa undertake their numerous official and private engagements. Maria Te-

tier et sa famille vivent au château de Fischbach, près de Mersch, où le couple princier s'acquitte de ses nombreux devoirs officiels et privés. Les activités quotidiennes de Maria Teresa comportent des tâches aussi variées que surveiller de près l'éducation des enfants, conduire Alexandra et Sébastien à l'école, prendre le petit déjeuner avec Guillaume, Félix et Louis, recevoir des associations en audience au palais grand-ducal ou organiser la réunion mensuelle de la Fondation Prince Henri – Princesse Maria Teresa. ◆ Pendant ce temps, le prince Henri se consacre essentiellement à ses fonctions officielles, à l'étude de ses dossiers et au traitement de sa correspondance. À ces occupations s'ajoutent les voyages effectués par le couple à l'occasion d'une réunion du comité directeur de la Fondation Mentor à Genève ou d'une mission économique, par exemple, ainsi que les séances de travail avec le maréchal de la Cour. Les activités privées de Maria Teresa comprennent l'organisation et la programmation domestiques du château de Fischbach, la mise au point hebdomadaire des tâches avec le personnel ou la composition du menu d'un dîner de gala. Le couple princier profite également de ses loisirs pour déjeuner de temps à autre en tête à tête en ville ou pour se rendre ensemble au théâtre ou au cinéma. ◆ Cet emploi

von Mersch, von wo aus das erbgroßherzogliche Paar seinen zahlreichen offiziellen und privaten Verpflichtungen nachkommt. Zu den täglichen Aufgaben von Maria Teresa gehören so unterschiedliche Bereiche wie die ständige erzieherische Überwachung der Kinder, die gemeinsame Fahrt zur Schule mit Alexandra und Sébastien, das gemeinsame Frühstück mit Guillaume, Félix und Louis, Audienzen im großherzoglichen Palais für humanitäre Organisationen oder die monatliche Sitzung der „Fondation Prince Henri-Princesse Maria Teresa". ◆ Währenddessen ist der Zeitplan von Prinz Henri geprägt von seinen offiziellen Funktionen, dem Aktenstudium oder der Aufarbeitung der Korrespondenz. Dazu kommen noch die gemeinsamen Reisen des Paares zum Beispiel im Rahmen einer Vorstandssitzung der Mentor-Stiftung nach Genf oder einer Wirtschaftsmission sowie die Arbeitssitzungen mit dem Hofmarschall. Zu den häuslichen Arbeiten von Maria Teresa gehören die hausinterne Organisation und Planung von Schloß Fischbach, die wöchentliche Abstimmung mit dem Personal oder die Zusammenstellung der Speisekarte für einen abendlichen Empfang. Die freie Zeit nutzt das erbgroßherzogliche Paar dann auch ab und zu für ein gemeinsames Mittagessen in der Stadt Luxemburg oder sie gehen abends

resa's everyday tasks include normal parental control of her children, taking Alexandra and Sébastien to school, breakfast together with Guillaume, Félix and Louis and audiences in the grand ducal palace for humanitarian organizations; there are also the monthly meetings of the Prince Henri-Princess Maria Teresa Foundation. ◆ Meanwhile, Prince Henri's timetable is determined by his official functions, the study of files or his correspondence. Then there are the joint engagements undertaken by the couple, for instance in connection with a board meeting of the Mentor Foundation in Geneva or a trade mission or else the working sessions with the Lord Chamberlain. Maria Teresa's domestic duties include the organization and planning of life in the Château de Fischbach, weekly briefing sessions for the staff and drawing up the menu for evening receptions. The couple also occasionally use their free time to have lunch together in Luxembourg city or to visit the theatre or cinema in the evening. ◆ This highly varied daily timetable with its wide range of duties is given a certain regularity and essential routine by annual family events held with the children's grandparents, by family outings and picnics on Sundays and by the children's weekly fencing, tennis, karate and riding lessons and last but not least by the

du temps très varié et rythmé par les tâches les plus diverses acquiert une certaine régularité et le côté routinier nécessaire grâce aux fêtes familiales annuelles avec les grands-parents, aux excursions et pique-niques dominicaux avec les enfants et aux séances hebdomadaires d'escrime, de tennis, de karaté et d'équitation des petits princes, sans oublier les vacances que la famille du grand-duc héritier passe chaque année partiellement avec le grand-duc Jean et la grande-duchesse Joséphine-Charlotte.

zusammen ins Theater oder ins Kino. ❖ Dieser sehr abwechslungsreiche und von den verschiedensten Aufgaben bestimmte Tagesablauf erhält eine gewisse Regelmäßigkeit und die notwendige Routine durch die alljährlichen Familienereignisse zusammen mit den Großeltern, die gemeinsamen Ausflüge und Picknicke mit den Kindern am Sonntag wie durch die wöchentlichen Fecht-, Tennis-, Karate- und Reitstunden der Kinder und nicht zuletzt auch die Ferien, die die erbgroßherzogliche Familie jedes Jahr zum Teil mit Großherzog Jean und Großherzogin Joséphine-Charlotte verbringt.

holidays each year, part of which the family spends with Grand Duke Jean and Grand Duchess Joséphine-Charlotte.

■ *Pages suivantes:* Photo de famille pour le 75ᵉ anniversaire du grand-duc Jean au château de Berg, en janvier 1996.

1 le prince Antoine de Ligne, 2 la princesse Alix de Ligne, 3 la princesse Marie-Gabrielle, comtesse de Holstein-Ledreborg, 4 le comte Knud de Holstein-Ledreborg, 5 le comte Carl-Joseph Henckel de Donnersmarck, 6 la princesse Marie-Adélaïde, comtesse Henckel de Donnersmarck, 7 la reine Paola, 8 le roi Albert II, 9 la reine Fabiola, 10 la princesse Elisabeth, duchesse de Hohenberg, 11 la princesse Maria Teresa, 12 le prince Henri et leurs enfants 27 la princesse Alexandra, 28 le prince Sébastien, 29 le prince Félix, 30 le prince Guillaume, 31 le prince Louis; 13 le grand-duc Jean, 14 la grande-duchesse Joséphine-Charlotte, 15 la princesse Marie-Astrid, 16 l'archiduc Christian d'Autriche et leurs enfants 32 la princesse Marie-Christine, 33 la princesse Gabriella, 34 le prince Imre, 35 le prince Christophe, 36 le prince Alexander; 17 la comtesse Hélène, 18 le prince Jean et leurs enfants 23 le comte Carl-Johann, 24 la comtesse Marie-Gabrielle, 25 le comte Constantin, 26 le comte Wenceslas; 19 la princesse Margaretha, 20 le prince Nicolas de Liechtenstein et leurs enfants 37 le prince Joseph-Emmanuel, 38 la princesse Maria-Annunciata, 39 la princesse Marie-Astrid, 21 le prince Guillaume, 22 la princesse Sibilla.

▫ *Auf den folgenden Seiten:* Familienfoto zum 75. Geburtstag von Großherzog Jean auf Schloß Berg im Januar 1996

1 Prinz Antoine de Ligne, 2 Prinzessin Alix de Ligne, 3 Prinzessin Marie-Gabrielle, Gräfin von Holstein-Ledreborg, 4 Graf Knud von Holstein-Ledreborg, 5 Graf Carl-Joseph Henckel von Donnersmarck, 6 Prinzessin Marie-Adélaïde, Gräfin Henckel von Donnersmarck, 7 Königin Paola, 8 König Albert II., 9 Königin Fabiola, 10 Prinzessin Elisabeth, Herzogin von Hohenberg; 11 Prinzessin Maria Teresa, 12 Prinz Henri und ihre Kinder 27 Prinzessin Alexandra, 28 Prinz Sébastien, 29 Prinz Félix, 30 Prinz Guillaume, 31 Prinz Louis; 13 Großherzog Jean, 14 Großherzogin Joséphine-Charlotte, 15 Prinzessin Marie-Astrid, 16 Erzherzog Christian von Österreich und ihre Kinder 32 Prinzessin Marie-Christine, 33 Prinzessin Gabriella, 34 Prinz Imre, 35 Prinz Christoph, 36 Prinz Alexander; 17 Gräfin Hélène, 18 Prinz Jean und ihre Kinder 23 Graf Carl-Johann, 24 Gräfin Marie-Gabrielle, 25 Graf Constantin, 26 Graf Wenceslas; 19 Prinzessin Margaretha, 20 Prinz Nikolaus von Liechtenstein und ihre Kinder 37 Prinz Josef-Emmanuel, 38 Prinzessin Maria-Annunciata, 39 Prinzessin Marie-Astrid; 21 Prinz Guillaume, 22 Prinzessin Sibilla.

■ *Following pages:* Family photograph taken on the 75th birthday of Grand Duke Jean at the Château de Berg, January 1996.

1 Prince Antoine of Ligne; 2 Princess Alix of Ligne; 3 Princess Marie-Gabrielle, Countess of Holstein-Ledreborg; 4 Count Knud of Holstein-Ledreborg; 5 Count Carl-Joseph Henckel of Donnersmarck; 6 Princess Marie-Adélaïde, Countess Henckel of Donnersmarck; 7 Queen Paola; 8 King Albert II; 9 Queen Fabiola; 10 Princess Elisabeth, Duchess of Hohenberg; 11 Princess Maria Teresa, 12 Prince Henri and their children: 27 Princess Alexandra, 28 Prince Sébastien, 29 Prince Félix, 30 Prince Guillaume and 31 Prince Louis; 13 Grand Duke Jean; 14 Grand Duchess Joséphine-Charlotte; 15 Princess Marie-Astrid, 16 Archduke Christian of Austria and their children: 32 Princess Marie-Christine, 33 Princess Gabriella, 34 Prince Imre, 35 Prince Christoph and 36 Prince Alexander; 17 Countess Hélène, 18 Prince Jean and their children: 23 Count Carl-Johann, 24 Countess Marie-Gabrielle, 25 Count Constantin and 26 Count Wenceslas; 19 Princess Margaretha, 20 Prince Nikolaus of Liechtenstein and their children: 37 Prince Josef-Emmanuel, 38 Princess Maria-Annunciata and 39 Princess Marie-Astrid; 21 Prince Guillaume, 22 Princess Sibilla.

Septembre 1988. Comme chaque année, la famille princière goûte aux plaisirs de la *Schueberfouer* qui perpétue la foire annuelle instaurée en 1340 par Jean l'Aveugle, comte de Luxembourg et roi de Bohème.

September 1988. Wie jedes Jahr, stattet die Prinzenfamilie der *Schueberfouer* einen Besuch ab. Die Schobermesse wurde 1340 von Johann dem Blinden, Graf von Luxemburg und König von Böhmen, ins Leben gerufen.

September 1988. Every year the family samples the pleasures of the *Schueberfouer*, which perpetuates the annual fair established in 1340 by John, Count of Luxembourg and King of Bohemia.

■ *Pages précédentes:*
En compagnie de ses labradors Yvi et Nara, le prince Henri visite la forêt de Fischbach après l'ouragan qui a ravagé la forêt luxembourgeoise en février 1990. La forêt couvre un tiers du territoire du grand-duché et a valu au Luxembourg le nom de département des Forêts pendant l'annexion à la France sous la Révolution et l'Empire (1795-1814).

■ *Auf den vorherigen Seiten:*
Nach den verheerenden Stürmen, die im Februar 1990 Luxemburgs Wälder verwüsteten, besucht Prinz Henri (hier in Begleitung seiner beiden Labradorhunde Yvi und Nara) den Wald von Schloß Fischbach. Daß ein Drittel des Großherzogtums bewaldet ist, trug Luxemburg bei der Annexion durch Frankreich (1795-1814) den Namen *département des Forêts* ein.

■ *Previous pages:*
Accompanied by his labradors Yvi and Nara, Prince Henri inspects the Fischbach forestry after the storms which ravaged the forests of Luxembourg in February 1990. One-third of the territory of the Grand Duchy is afforested, which earned Luxembourg the name *département des Forêts* during the period of annexation to France under the revolutionary regime and the Empire (1795-1814).

■ Printemps 1990.
Dans les jardins de Fischbach la grande-duchesse héritière peut se livrer à sa passion du jardinage et se détendre avec ses enfants Louis, Guillaume et Félix.

■ Frühling 1990.
In den Gärten von Fischbach kann sich die Erbgroßherzogin ihrer Leidenschaft, der Gartenarbeit, widmen und sich mit ihren Kindern Louis, Guillaume und Félix entspannen.

■ Spring 1990.
In the Fischbach gardens Princess Maria Teresa is able to indulge her passion for gardening and to relax with her children Louis, Guillaume and Félix.

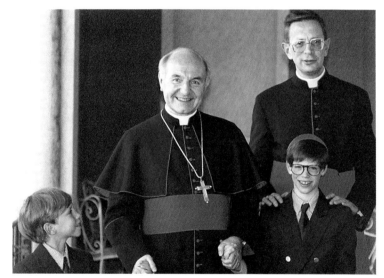

■ Voyage privé au Vatican en 1993 au cours duquel le prince Louis
a reçu sa première communion des mains du Saint-Père

■ Privatreise 1993 in den Vatikan, wo Prinz Louis die Erstkommunion
aus den Händen des Heiligen Vaters erhält

■ Private trip to the Vatican in 1993, during which Prince Louis
received his First Communion from the Holy Father

■ Voyage en Russie, novembre 1989

▨ Rußlandreise im November 1989

■ Visiting Russia, November 1989

Saint-Nicolas 1984.
À Luxembourg, Saint-Nicolas distribue des jouets aux enfants sages le 6 décembre tandis que le terrible Père Fouettard se charge de punir les enfants désobéissants. Le prince Guillaume fait visiblement partie des premiers.

St.-Nikolaus-Tag 1984.
In Luxemburg erhalten brave Kinder am 6. Dezember Spielzeug vom Sankt Nikolaus; ungehorsame Kinder dagegen werden von Knecht Ruprecht bestraft. Prinz Guillaume gehört eindeutig zu ersteren...

Saint Nicholas' Day, 1984.
In Luxembourg, Saint Nicholas hands out presents to good children on 6 December, while the Bogeyman, le Père Fouettard, stands by with his switch to deal with the naughty ones. Prince Guillaume is clearly one of the former.

Noël 1996 au château de Fischbach. On reconnaît, de gauche à droite, sur la photo du haut, le prince Félix, la princesse Alexandra et les princes Sébastien, Guillaume et Louis.

Weihnachten 1996 auf Schloß Fischbach. Von links nach rechts, auf dem oberen Foto: Prinz Félix, Prinzessin Alexandra und die Prinzen Sébastien, Guillaume und Louis.

Christmas 1996 in the Château de Fischbach. In the top photograph, left to right, are Prince Félix, Princess Alexandra and the Princes Sébastien, Guillaume and Louis.

■ Un jeune couple épanoui tant dans sa vie officielle
que dans sa vie familiale

■ Ein strahlendes junges Paar im offiziellen
wie im privaten Leben

■ A radiant young couple in public
as well as in private

■ Avec Yehudi. Menuhin à Wiltz.
Chez Jean-Claude Biver, de Blancpain, à Lausanne 1995.

▨ Mit Yehudi Menuhin in Wiltz.
1995 bei Jean-Claude Biver von Blancpain in Lausanne.

■ With Yehudi Menuhin at Wiltz.
Visiting Jean-Claude Biver of the Blancpain company in Lausanne, 1995.

■ Marc Girardelli à Fischbach, 1994.
Avec Luciano Pavarotti à la Scala de Milan, en décembre 1985.

▨ Marc Girardelli in Fischbach, 1994.
Mit Luciano Pavarotti in der Mailänder Scala, Dezember 1985.

■ Marc Girardelli at Fischbach, 1994.
With Luciano Pavarotti at La Scala in Milan, December 1985.

■ Avec M. et Mme Kofi
Annan, secrétaire
général de l'ONU,
au forum mondial
de Davos, 1997.

En compagnie
de Peter Ustinov,
lors de la soirée de la
King's Cup à Phuket
en décembre 1996.

Avec Clint Eastwood,
maire de Carmel,
Californie,
en septembre 1987.

La princesse reçoit
soeur Emmanuelle
au Cercle municipal
de Luxembourg.

■ Mit UNO-
Generalsekretär
Kofi Annan und dessen
Ehefrau beim
Weltwirtschaftsforum
1997 in Davos.

In Begleitung von
Peter Ustinov beim
Empfang des King's Cup
in Phuket, Dezember
1996.

Mit dem Bürgermeister
von Carmel,
Clint Eastwood,
im September 1987
in Kalifornien.

Die Prinzessin empfängt
Schwester Emmanuelle
im hauptstädtischen
Cercle municipal.

■ With Kofi Annan,
Secretary-General of the
United Nations, and his
wife at the Davos World
Forum in 1997.

In the company of
Peter Ustinov at the
King's Cup reception in
Phuket, December 1996.

With Clint Eastwood,
Mayor of Carmel,
California,
in September 1987.

The Princess welcomes
Sister Emmanuelle
to the Luxembourg
Cercle municipal.

■ Après l'école, les petits princes peuvent s'ébattre dans le parc du château de Fischbach.
Sur la photo de droite: Louis, 10 ans, Alexandra, 6 ans, Guillaume, 15 ans, Sébastien, 5 ans et Félix, 13 ans.

■ Nach der Schule toben die Prinzenkinder im Park von Schloß Fischbach.
Auf dem Foto von rechts: Louis (10 Jahre), Alexandra (6 Jahre), Guillaume (15 Jahre); Sébastien (5 Jahre) und Félix (13 Jahre).

■ After school, the young Princes and Princess are able to play in the grounds of the Château de Fischbach.
The photograph on the right shows Louis (10), Alexandra (6), Guillaume (15), Sébastien (5) and Félix (13).

■ *Pages précedentes:*
Malgré les tâches officielles,
la grande-duchesse héritière ne néglige pas ses
rôles de mère de famille et de maîtresse de maison

■ *Auf den vorherigen Seiten:*
Trotz ihrer zahlreichen offiziellen Verpflichtungen
vernachlässigt die Erbgroßherzogin ihre Aufgaben
als Familienmutter und Hausherrin nicht

■ *Previous pages:*
Despite her official duties, Princess Maria Teresa
does not neglect her roles as a mother and
housewife

■ Les plaisirs de la vie à la campagne

■ Die Freuden des Landlebens

■ The pleasures of country life

■ Une famille d'aujourd'hui: il arrive que Maman travaille à son bureau
pendant que Papa initie Alexandra aux jeux sur ordinateur

□ Eine Familie von heute: Es kommt schon einmal vor, daß Mama im Büro arbeitet,
während Papa Alexandra Computerspiele beibringt

■ A modern family. It can happen that Mum works at her desk
while Dad explains a computer game to Alexandra.

Une famille sportive.
Le prince Félix au karaté,
le prince Louis à l'escrime
et les princes Guillaume
et Félix au tennis.

Eine sportliche Familie:
Prinz Félix beim Karate-Training,
Prinz Louis beim Fechten und
die Prinzen Guillaume und Félix
beim Tennisspiel.

A sporting family.
Prince Félix doing karate,
Prince Louis fencing and
Princes Guillaume and Félix
playing tennis.

St-Moritz 1996

Vendanges 1996 à Greiveldange. Le vignoble luxembourgeois occupe
plus de 1.300 ha sur les coteaux et les terrasses de la vallée de la Moselle
et produit annuellement 150.000 hl de vins blancs, dont la moitié est exportée.

Weinlese 1996 in Greiveldingen. Luxemburgs Weinberge an den Hängen
der Mosel nehmen über 1300 Hektar ein und liefern jährlich 150.000 Hektoliter
Weißwein, von dem rund die Hälfte exportiert wird.

■ The 1996 grape harvest at Greiveldange. The Luxembourg vineyards occupy more than 1,300 hectares of the slopes and terraces of the Moselle valley and produce fifteen million litres of white wine every year, half of which is exported.

■ Phuket, décembre 1996. À l'occasion du cinquantième anniversaire
du roi Bhumibol de Thaïlande, le prince Henri participe à la traditionnelle
King's Cup à bord du *Sturmvogel*.

■ Phuket im Dezember 1996. Anläßlich des 50. Geburtstags von König Bhumipol
von Thailand nimmt Prinz Henri an Bord des *Sturmvogel* am traditionellen
King's Cup teil.

■ Phuket, December 1996, on the occasion of the fiftieth birthday
of King Bhumibol of Thailand, Prince Henri competes in the traditional
King's Cup on board the *Sturmvogel*

■ Voyage de noces aux Bahamas en 1981.
Le prince Guillaume aux îles Galapagos en 1987.

▨ Flitterwochen 1981 auf den Bahamas.
Prinz Guillaume 1987 auf den Galapagos-Inseln.

■ Honeymoon in the Bahamas in 1981.
Prince Guillaume on the Galapagos in 1987.

■ La princesse Maria Teresa avec Sébastien et Alexandra à Cabasson en 1996.

Le couple princier avec Guillaume, Louis et Félix à Cabasson en 1990.

Félix, Guillaume et Louis à Eurodisney en 1993.

Page de droite:
Le grand-duc héritier avec Alexandra et Sébastien à Cabasson en 1994.

▨ Prinzessin Maria Teresa mit Sébastien und Alexandra 1996 in Cabasson.

Das Prinzenpaar 1990 mit Guillaume, Louis und Félix in Cabasson.

Félix, Guillaume und Louis 1993 im „Eurodisney" bei Paris.

Rechte Seite:
Der Erbgroßherzog mit Alexandra und Sébastien 1994 in Cabasson.

■ Princess Maria Teresa with Sébastien and Alexandra at Cabasson in 1996.

The Prince and Princess with Guillaume, Louis and Félix at Cabasson in 1990.

Félix, Guillaume and Louis at Eurodisney in 1993.

Right page:
The Heir Apparent with Alexandra and Sébastien at Cabasson in 1994.

■ Vacances en Grèce, 1996

□ Urlaub 1996 in Griechenland

■ Holidays in Greece, 1996

■ La formation des jeunes princes inclut également
le sport, la musique et des visites culturelles

▨ Zur Ausbildung der jungen Prinzen gehören
auch Sport, Musik und Besuche kultureller
Veranstaltungen

■ The education of the young princes and princess
also includes sport, music and cultural outings

143

Photos de famille. Avril 1994.
De g. à dr.: la princesse Margaretha
et le prince Nicolas de Liechtenstein,
la comtesse Hélène de Nassau et le prince Jean, la
princesse Sibilla et le prince Guillaume,
la princesse Maria Teresa et le prince Henri,
la princesse Marie-Astrid et l'archiduc Christian
d'Autriche.

page de droite:
Septembre 1994.
De g. à dr.: les princes Sébastien, Alexandra,
Louis, Félix et Guillaume.

Familienfotos. April 1994.
V.l.n.r.: Prinzessin Margaretha und Prinz Nikolaus
von Liechtenstein, Gräfin Hélène von Nassau und
Prinz Jean, Prinzessin Sibilla und Prinz Guillaume,
Prinzessin Maria Teresa und Prinz Henri,
Prinzessin Marie-Astrid und Erzherzog Christian
von Österreich.

Rechte Seite:
September 1994.
V.l.n.r.: die Prinzen Sébastien, Alexandra, Louis,
Félix und Guillaume.

Family photos. April 1994.
Left to right, Princess Margaretha and
Prince Nikolaus of Liechtenstein,
Countess Hélène of Nassau and Prince Jean,
Princess Sibilla and Prince Guillaume,
Princess Maria Teresa and Prince Henri,
Princess Marie-Astrid and Archduke Christian
of Austria.

Right:
September 1994.
Left to right, Prince Sébastien, Princess Alexandra
and the Princes Louis, Félix and Guillaume.

Pages précédentes:
Les petits princes avec leurs grands-parents
et leur arrière-grand-mère, la grande-duchesse
Charlotte

Vorherige Seiten:
Die Prinzenkinder mit ihren Großeltern
und ihrer Urgroßmutter, Großherzogin Charlotte

Previous pages:
The young princes and princess with their
grandparents and their great-grandmother, Grand-
Duchess Charlotte

Cabasson, 1990.
Le prince Henri avec ses frères et soeurs
Margaretha, Guillaume, Jean et Marie-Astrid.

Voyage aux îles Galapagos, 1987.

La grande muraille, avril 1988.

Page de gauche:
Arabie-Saoudite, décembre 1995,
excursion dans le désert près de Riad.

Cabasson, 1990.
Prinz Henri mit seinen Geschwistern Margaretha,
Guillaume, Jean und Marie-Astrid.

Reise zu den Galapagos-Inseln, 1987.

Die Chinesische Mauer, April 1988.

Linke Seite:
Ausflug in die Wüste bei Riad (Saudi-Arabien)
im Dezember 1995.

Cabasson, 1990.
Prince Henri with his brothers and sisters
Margaretha, Guillaume, Jean and Marie-Astrid.

Visiting the Galapagos, 1987.

The Great Wall of China, April 1988.

Left:
Saudi Arabia, December 1995. In the desert
near Riyadh.

■ Les premières années d'un futur prince héritier

▓ Die ersten Jahre eines angehenden Erbprinzen

■ The first years of a future Heir Apparent